STUDIES IN HISTORY, ECONOMICS, AND PUBLIC LAW

EDITED BY THE FACULTY OF POLITICAL SCIENCE
OF COLUMBIA UNIVERSITY

Number 321

ETHICAL TEACHINGS IN THE LATIN HYMNS OF
MEDIEVAL ENGLAND

ETHICAL TEACHINGS IN THE LATIN HYMNS OF MEDIEVAL ENGLAND

With special reference to the seven deadly sins and the seven principal virtues

BY

RUTH ELLIS MESSENGER, Ph. D.

NEW YORK
COLUMBIA UNIVERSITY PRESS
LONDON: P. S. KING & SON, LTD.
1930

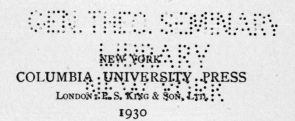

COPYRIGHT, 1930

BY

COLUMBIA UNIVERSITY PRESS

PRINTED IN THE UNITED STATES OF AMERICA

IN MEMORIAM

WILLIAM EVERETT WATERS

SOMETIME PROFESSOR OF GREEK

NEW YORK UNIVERSITY

ACKNOWLEDGMENT

THE author wishes to acknowledge her indebtedness to all those who, by advice, criticism and encouragement have helped to make possible the following study. Her thanks are due more particularly to Professor Austin P. Evans of Columbia University and Professor William W. Rockwell of Union Theological Seminary under whose joint direction and with whose continued aid the study has been pursued. The author is also grateful for many courtesies extended by the librarians and their assistants at Cornell University, Williams College, New York Public Library, General Theological Seminary, Columbia University and Union Theological Seminary. Finally, she welcomes the opportunity to express her gratitude to those personal friends whose interest in this task has been an unfailing source of inspiration.

RUTH ELLIS MESSENGER.

NEW YORK CITY, OCTOBER 1, 1929.

7

TABLE OF ABBREVIATIONS

CSEL   *Corpus Scriptorum Ecclesiasticorum Latinorum.*
PG   *Patrologiae Cursus Completus, Series Graeca.* Migne.
PL   *Patrologiae Cursus Completus, Series Latina.* Migne.

The editions of service books used as a basis for this study have been abbreviated as follows:

S.M.   *Sarum Missal,* edited by F. H. Dickinson (Oxford: Pitsligo Press, 1861-1883).

S.B.   *Sarum Breviary,* edited by F. Procter and C. Wordsworth (Canterbury: Academy, 1879-1886).

S.P.   *Sarum Processional,* edited by W. G. Henderson (Leeds: M'Corquodale, 1882).

Y.M.   *York Missal,* edited by W. G. Henderson, Surtees Soc. Pub., vols. 59, 60, 1874.

Y.B.   *York Breviary,* edited by S. W. Lawley, Surtees Soc. Pub., vols 71, 75, 1880-1883.

Y.P.   *York Processional,* edited by W. G. Henderson, Surtees Soc. Pub., vol. 63, 1875.

H.M.   *Hereford Missal,* edited by W. G. Henderson (Leeds: M'Corquodale, 1874).

H.B.   *Hereford Breviary,* edited by W. H. Frere and E. G. Brown, Henry Bradshaw Soc. Pub. (London: 1904, 1911).

D.H.   *Latin Hymns of the Anglo-Saxon Church,* edited by J. Stevenson, Surtees Soc. Pub., vol. 23, 1851. This is the *Durham Hymnarium.*

W.T.   *Tropary of Ethelred,* Surtees Soc. Pub., vol. 60. (Published as an appendix to the *York Missal.*) This is the *Winchester Troper.*

Anal. Hymn. *Analecta Hymnica Medii Aevi,* vols. 50, 51. These contain the additional hymns chosen from Mearns' Index.

TABLE OF CONTENTS

INTRODUCTION

" The works of the religious lyric poetry give us an instructive picture of the culture and spiritual life of the early Christian Age and of the Middle Ages."

This brief statement by the Rev. Clemens Blume, S.J., in an article in the Catholic Encyclopedia on *Hymnody* suggests the theme which has been pursued in the following pages. It is further elaborated in another essay by the same author, *Hymnologie und Kulturgeschichte des Mittelalters,* as follows: " Above all, the history of hymnody must be, and if rightly understood, will be, a history of culture of a special kind, a history of ideas and ideals as the Christian west from the fourth to the sixteenth century has clothed them in the form of poetry, sometimes mediocre, sometimes brilliant." [1]

That the hymns of the medieval church reflect in a very striking manner the point of view of the period, is true not only in a general way but in many special phases of medieval culture. Ideas of the cosmos, allegory and typology, celestial hierarchies, demonology, mysticism, miracle, cults of saints, standards of life and conduct, all have their place in this body of literature. An attempt will be made to separate certain of these strands from the texture of the religious poetry, which in its turn will be conceived as a part of the larger pattern of medieval life. That phase which concerns ethical ideals and standards of conduct as revealed in hymns has been selected from the many possible lines of inquiry.

One learns from the hymns the nature of the approved life and the moral standards which commended themselves to the age. Terms of praise or blame, the exalting of great virtues,

[1] *Festschrift Georg von Hertling* (Kempten: Kösel'sche Buchhandlung, 1913), p. 119.

the repudiation of hated sins, admiration expressed for one
individual, loathing for another, all help to reveal the ideal
man or woman of medieval thought. The ideals of conduct
which emerge as such a study proceeds, are neither vague nor
formless. Emphasis upon certain virtues and certain sins is
repeated and insistent. It seems clear that the authors of
hymns had in mind, chiefly, the seven principal virtues and
the seven deadly sins of medieval teaching. Faith, hope,
love, moderation, justice, wisdom, and bravery accompany
the ideal character, while pride, avarice, impurity, wrath,
gluttony, envy and sloth are hateful to it.

The materials for the study of ideas and ideals as revealed
in Latin hymns are abundant. In the essay by Father Blume
to which reference has been made, he traces the progress of
hymnological study from the beginning and expresses the
opinion that the work of editing and criticism has now
reached the stage where students of culture may use the
materials provided advantageously. An extensive literature
exists relating to medieval Latin hymnology, including for
the most part editions of the sources, critical treatments of
authorship and dates of composition, collections of hymns of
one author or period, histories of medieval Latin literature,
and studies of meters, music and liturgy. Aside from scattered investigations of special hymns, however, or of the
work of individual hymn writers, the relation of this body
of material to medieval culture has been neglected. The
present study treats only the cultural aspect and is built upon
the foundations of editorial and textual criticism laid by
others. Problems connected with metrical form or musical
setting will be omitted.

With so much material at one's disposal it has been difficult
to determine the most suitable for the present purpose.
From among the great liturgical collections which grew up in
various parts of medieval Europe, the hymns of certain im-

portant English liturgies have been selected, especially those
of Sarum, because of their highly representative character,
the careful editing of the service books in which they are contained, the fact that their widespread use can be proved, and
finally, the availability of the collections in printed form.   In
the first chapter of this essay, the collections have been described and an attempt has been made to justify their selection as a basis for the study of cultural history.

It will also be necessary to test the validity of Father
Blume's position that medieval Latin hymns reflect the contemporary point of view concerning ideas and ideals.   This
can be done in a general way through a comparison of various media of expression.   If some particular ethical conception, for instance, is apparent in the hymns, it should be
discoverable in other forms of medieval literature, secular or
religious, in the drama and in art.   It should be illustrated in
the sermon, legend, romance, in sculpture and stained glass.
Where harmony of thought and opinion is found in such a
variety of forms, the hymn may be trusted as being truly
representative of the ethical point of view.   As a matter of
fact, in every case where hymns have been thus tested in the
following pages, a most interesting correspondence of ideas
is observable.

Even if it be granted for the above reasons, that the use of
hymns is justified as a reflection of thought, some may question their suitability on the ground that the meaning of
the hymn is formally expressed.   Traditional phraseology,
conventional formulas, possibly a certain degree of cant, con-
spire to impair the significance of the thought.   It must be
admitted that medieval hymns are not altogether exempt from
this criticism, especially after the thirteenth century, but
it must also be admitted that conventional forms, when employed, are likely to be of the essence of medieval religious
ideas.   The obscuring factor is often more apparent than

real, particularly when one recalls the long process of selection to which liturgical hymns were subjected.   Only those
truly representative were able to maintain their position in
the ritual of the church.   Again, the supposedly conventional
formula may be expressive of some eternal verity of the
Christian faith, common alike to all ages of Christian history.
Ideals and doctrines prove to be, upon closer examination,
not exclusively medieval but at all times, Christian.   But in
spite of similarities which arise from the expression of beliefs
fundamental to Christianity in all ages, medieval hymns differ
greatly from those of modern times.

The simplest way to convince oneself that Christian hymns
of all periods are not all alike, in spite of certain omnipresent
forms, is to place a few representative recent hymns side by
side with the medieval.   The hymnology of Protestantism
as well as of Catholicism has been greatly enriched within
modern times by the addition of many pieces voicing the
aspirations of our own day.   For Protestantism, one may
point out the " revival " hymn, the missionary hymn and the
hymn of social service.   For Catholicism, the hymns of men
like Newman, Caswall and Faber have found a place in
hymnals and books of devotion.   Among contributions to
Protestant hymnology, perhaps the most interesting of the
three types just mentioned is the last, in which the realization
of the kingdom of God upon earth is the basic thought.   It
may be argued, of course, that the practice of benevolent
deeds by saints, as recounted in medieval hymns, corresponds
somewhat to the modern ideal of altruism.[1]   Such hymns
illustrate the performance of those almsdeeds which were
known to the people of the Middle Ages as the seven works
of mercy, and are to this day the expression for the Catholic,

[1] *Promere chorda*, W.T., for St. Martin; *Plaudat chorus plebs laetetur*,
Y.M., for St. William; *Gaudeamus Messia*, S.M., for St. Osmund; *Alma
cohors una*, S.M., for Common of Confessors.

of the ideal of love to man. To feed the hungry, to give
drink to the thirsty, to clothe the naked, to harbor the harbor-
less, to visit the sick, to ransom the captive and to bury the
dead, constitute the corporal works of mercy. The spiritual
works of mercy require the Christian to instruct the ignorant, to counsel the doubtful, to admonish sinners, to bear
wrongs patiently, to forgive offenses willingly, to comfort
the afflicted and to pray for the living and the dead. Among
the saints who embodied the high ideal which is set by these
obligations, are St. Laurence and St. Nicholas, whose generosity to the poor will be discussed in another connection;
St. Martin, famous for sharing his cloak with a beggar; St.
William of York, St. Osmund and other great bishops and
confessors, conspicuous for acts of love which carried with
them both material and spiritual aid. Such illustrations
might be multiplied, not only in connection with the social
motive but in many other instances where the hymnology
of different periods is found to be closely in harmony with
ideas of a particular age. If then, conventional expressions
appropriate to all Christian hymns are set aside, there still
remain the ideas which may be considered more strictly
medieval or aspects of thought appearing in the medieval
stage of their evolution. This is clearly the case in the field
of ethical ideas, where virtues and sins common to humanity
at all times are described in terms of a medieval concept.

Another objection to the use of hymns as illustrative of the
thought of the Middle Ages is based upon the fact that they
were written in the language of the learned class, in a word
that they represent the opinion of churchmen and not of the
people at large. The question of the actual participation of
the illiterate classes in the rites of their religion will be considered presently. It may be pointed out here that the leading ideas conveyed by the hymnology of the church were
communicated even to the most uneducated groups by the

dramatic element in the liturgy, by pictures, images and relics, by instructions and devotions in the vernacular, by processions and festivals and by sermons of friars and other medieval preachers. Of course not all these devices were necessarily synchronous but they were all employed at one time or another. Again, it is highly probable that more of the actual Latin words were understood than is popularly supposed, from the twelfth century on to the close of the Middle Ages. This is suggested, at least, by the free use of Latin in goliard village entertainments, by the extraordinary popularity of Latin parodies on certain hymns, by poems in which Latin and a vernacular are combined, by the survival of many Latin phrases and sentences in medieval drama, and by references to hymns in vernacular literature.

A detailed study of the problem as to the extent of popular acquaintance with Latin in the later medieval centuries, is impossible here. Only a few illustrations can be given of the evidence which is available along the lines just indicated. These have been selected from material closely related to hymnology since the question at issue concerns the capacity of the people at large to understand Latin hymns.

The subject of goliardic poetry has received considerable attention. Its origin, authorship, and place in medieval literature and society have often been discussed. The point of contact between student songs and the problem of acquaintance with Latin lies in the audience entertained by the wandering singer. This poetry had appeared first in the eleventh or possibly the tenth century, reaching its widest influence in France in the twelfth century. It was composed after models furnished largely by hymnology. Whoever understood and appreciated student songs could understand hymns. Eliminating the clerical order, a far more inclusive group, by the way, than at present, who else may possibly have enjoyed the entertainment provided by the goliard or the songs that he spread throughout western Europe? Jusserand pictures him in the fourteenth century before an audience of nobles.[1] Allen declares that goliardic songs were sung in the streets.[2] If townsmen and knights as well as the members of the clergy composed the audiences of the wandering minstrel, they must have been able to catch the meaning of the Latin verse. Moreover, certain favorite poems of this kind were parodies on well-known Latin hymns. Perhaps the most popular was the drinking song *Vinum bonum et suave,* the variants of which, as Lehmann says are " too numerous to be mentioned " within the scope of his work on medieval parodies.[3] Had not the hymn *Verbum bonum et suave* been familiar to the hearers of the parody its force would have been lost. Other hymns which were frequently parodied were *Iam lucis orto sidere* and *Laetabundus exsultet—Regem regum.*[4]

The parody was not limited to Latin for the vernacular was sometimes combined with the Latin in the manner of macaronic verse, that is, verse in which vernacular words of one or more modern languages are intermixed with Latin words. Daniel prints a parody of *Aurora lucis rutilat* in German and Latin and a parody of *Laetabundus exsultet—Regem regum* in French with Latin refrains.[5]

Macaronic verse occurs in many other forms beside that of parody. Since a knowledge of both languages employed is necessary to carry on the thought, it indicates an acquaintance with Latin on the part of those who read or heard it. Several poems of this kind are found in the *Carmina Burana*

[1] J. J. Jusserand, *English Wayfaring Life in the Middle Ages* (London: Unwin, 1920), 2nd edition, p. 200.

[2] P. S. Allen, " Origins of the German Minnesang," *Modern Philology,* III (1906), p. 429.

[3] P. Lehmann, *Die Parodie im Mittelalter* (München: Drei Masken Verlag, 1922), pp. 174-178. Daniel, *Thesaurus Hymnologicus,* I, p. 282.

[4] Lehmann, *op. cit.,* pp. 119, 179.

[5] Daniel, *Thesaurus Hymnologicus,* I, p. 281; II, p. 62.

where French or German is the vernacular language used. The illustration which follows has been chosen from a different collection, *English Religious Lyrics of the XIVth Century*. It is entitled *Esto Memor Mortis*.

> Syth alle that in this wordle hath been *in rerum natura,*
> Or in this wyde wordle was seen *in humana cura,*
> Alle schalle passe with-outen ween *via mortis dura*;
> God graunte that mannys soule be cleen *penas non passura.*[1]

Other macaronic songs composed in England during the period of Middle English literature will be found noted in Brown's *Register.*[2]

When the medieval drama was removed from the precincts of the church to the market place it took on the form of vernacular speech. Sometimes the vernacular constituted a translation or paraphrase of the Latin.[3] At other times the Latin is blended with the vernacular in such a way that a knowledge of both is necessary for the full understanding of the text.   The first secular drama printed in Manly's *Specimens of the Pre-Shakespearean Drama* is the Norwich " Grocer's Play," *The Creation and Fall*. It opens with these lines : [4]

PATER : *Ego principium, Alpha et Omega, in altissimis habito:*
> In the hevenly empery I am resident.
It ys not semely for man, *sine adjutorio,*
> To be allone, nor very convenyent.   (lines 1-4)

Adam speaks thus of Eve a few lines further on:

[1] C. Brown, *English Religious Lyrics of the XIVth Century* (Oxford: Clarendon Press, 1924), no. 135.

[2] C. Brown, *Register of Middle English Religious and Didactic Verse* (Oxford: Univ. Press, 1920), nos. 3, 60, 247, 261, 319 *et seq.*

[3] E. K. Chambers, *Mediaeval Stage* (Oxford: Clarendon Press, 1903), II, pp. 88, 90.

[4] J. M. Manly, *Specimens of the Pre-Shaksperean Drama* (Boston: Ginn & Co., 1897).

ADAM : Thys creature to me ys *nunc ex ossibus meis*,
  And *virago* I call hyr in thy presens,
  Lyke on-to me in naturall preemynens.   (lines 19-21)

Such illustrations might be greatly multiplied.

References to hymns and the singing of hymns are rare in medieval secular literature, perhaps because hymns were common enough to be ignored. When they do occur, they are significant. Medieval readers of the vernacular translations of the *Golden Legend* were expected to understand such references as the following: " And therefore it is read in an hymn that he (St. Andrew) rendered the life to young men drowned in the sea." [1]

It seems reasonable to suppose, from evidence like the above, that a goodly proportion of the population of western Europe during the later Middle Ages, knew enough Latin to understand the hymns or else were acquainted with their teachings through vernacular media. If so, the use of hymns as a reflection of the thought of persons both within and without the learned class is justified. It happens moreover that for those who did not understand Latin many hymns existed in translation.

Translations and paraphrases of Latin hymns were common in England. The friars seem to have been the earliest translators of hymns into the vernacular for use in connection with preaching. William Herebert, a Franciscan, (d. 1333) is known to have rendered seventeen hymns and antiphons into English. Fourteen have been printed by Brown in his collection of fourteenth-century English lyrics. As might have been expected the leading hymns in the liturgy were the ones selected for translation. There are five additional hymns in English translation in Brown's collection. In the entire period covered by Brown's *Register* a large

---

[1] *Golden Legend* (Temple Classics), II, p. 99. *Vide* also the Assumption hymn quoted in volume iv, p. 245.

number of translations were made, as well as many paraphrases of Latin hymns.[1]   Attention should be called to the
fact that English lyric and didactic poetry at this time was
devoted very largely to instruction in matters of " faith,
morals and manners ".[2]   Consequently the teachings of Latin
hymns both in the reproductions of the original and in poems
employing similar subject matter, make it all the more likely
that the ethical lessons which they contained were familiar
everywhere.

Not alone were vernacular drama and hymn affected by
liturgical influence.   The liturgy became the inspiration of
much of the medieval religious poetry.   This subject has
been treated by Robert Stroppel in connection with German
poetry between the years 1050 and 1300.   The significance
of the liturgy has been pointed out by this author, not only
in the origin of religious poetry but as a background to all
medieval life.[3]   This consideration also has an important
bearing upon the question of how far Latin hymns were popularly understood.

Two of the problems pertinent to any discussion of medieval hymns as a reflection of medieval thought have now been
stated briefly, namely the question of the extent to which
hymns express opinions aside from conventional formulas,
and the question of acquaintance with Latin on the part of
those outside the ranks of the learned class, or else acquaintance with the same ideas in vernacular forms which are
nearly related to the Latin forms.   One more problem is
closely involved with these.   What can be said of the participation of the uneducated classes in medieval religious rites?

The subject of medieval popular religion, above all of rustic
religious ideas, is one that has claimed the attention of numer-

[1] Some fifty poems of this nature are listed in the *Register*.

[2] C. Brown, *Register*, II, pp. xiv-xv.

[3] R. Stroppel, *Liturgie und geistliche Dichtung zwischen 1050-1300*
(Frankfurt am Main: Diesterweg, 1927).

ous students of the Middle Ages. Various types of religious practice have been mentioned by means of which the illiterate classes of the period became acquainted with the ideas of their faith. " What did this jostling crew of citizens and rustics " make of it all?[1] For the present the better educated classes may be set aside. Scholarly opinion upon the subject of the religion of the illiterate masses of the Middle Ages, particularly the peasant, seems to be sharply divided. The attitude of Janssen who has described the religion of the German people in the pre-Reformation period, is highly optimistic as to the degree of religious education which they enjoyed.[2] Luchaire, on the other hand, pictures a medieval peasantry in France ignorant and neglected in matters of religious instruction.[5] More recent medievalists, such as Cardinal Gasquet and Professor Coulton, have interpreted the existing evidence upon the subject in a most divergent manner. It would be presumptuous to offer conclusions as the discussion stands today. All that can be done here is to survey briefly certain kinds of evidence bearing upon this subject, which support the position that medieval people of the uneducated classes received religious training in the elements of their faith, and had an opportunity to become familiar with the ideas which are expressed in medieval hymns.

Since this essay is concerned primarily with liturgical hymns used in England, the situation respecting religious

---

[1] G. H. Gerould, *Saints' Legends* (Boston: Houghton, Mifflin Co., 1916), p. 298.

[2] J. Janssen, *Geschichte des deutschen Volkes seit dem Ausgang des Mittelalters* (Freiburg im Breisgau: Herder, 1883-1894), 8 vols. This is translated as *History of the German People* (St. Louis: Herder, 1896), 16 vols. *Vide* also E. Michael, *Geschichte des deutschen Volkes seit dem 13. Jahrh. bis zum Ausgang des Mittelalters* (Freiburg: Herder, 1897-1915), 6 vols.

[3] A. Luchaire, *La Société française au temps de Philippe-Auguste* (Paris: Hachette, 1909). Trans. *Social France at the Time of Philip Augustus* (New York: Holt, 1912), from second edition.

training in the English parishes will receive the greater attention, while only incidental mention of French and central
European conditions will be made.

The first clue as to the character and extent of participation
in religious services and instruction during the Middle Ages
is offered by books of popular devotion and instruction, in
vernacular prose and poetry.   Certain of them were written
especially for the parish priest to aid him in his work with an
illiterate flock.   Others, combining dogma with illustrative
tales, were heard at village gatherings of a secular nature.
All of them are significant in this study, not only because of
their teachings concerning ethical ideals but because they
demonstrate the familiarity of a very large number of people
with the ideas which inspired the hymnology of the age.

Some years ago William Maskell made the following statement which he believed to be amply supported by evidence at
hand.   " For there never was a period in the history of the
English church when care was not taken to enforce upon all
priests the duty of teaching their people the rudiments of the
faith in the vulgar tongue and to provide books fitted for that
purpose." [1]   Of the evidence offered by Maskell, the Constitutions of Archbishop Peckham of Canterbury (the Canons of Lambeth IX-XIII), 1281, are extremely important.

*In quorum remedium discriminum statuendo Praecipimus, ut
quilibet sacerdos plebi praesidens quater in anno, hoc est, semel
in qualibet quarta anni, una die solenni vel pluribus, per se vel
per alium, exponat populo vulgariter absque cuiuslibet subtilitatis
textura fantastica XIIII Fidei articulos; X Mandata decalogi;
duo Praecepta evangelii, videlicet, geminae charitatis; et VII
etiam opera misericordia; VII capitalia peccata, cum sua
progenie; VII Virtutes principales; ac etiam VII Gratiae
sacramenta.* [2]

[1] W. Maskell, *Monumenta Ritualia Ecclesiae Anglicanae* (Oxford:
Clarendon Press, 1882), III, p. 1.

[2] Wilkins, *Concilia*, II, 54.   Also printed in *Lay Folks' Catechism*
(E.E.T.S., O.S., 118), pp. 7, 21.

Clearly the effectiveness of the decrees of Archbishop Peckham or of any other church official depended upon their enforcement. Whether the instructions were carefully followed in this case cannot be determined but there is a certain amount of evidence which points in that direction. Cardinal Gasquet mentions a diocesan synod (c. 1350) which ordered the enforcement of the Peckham Constitutions.[1] The cooperation of Archbishop Thoresby of York, which will be explained below, was very effective. The Synod of Ely, 1364, virtually repeated Peckham's instructions. In 1408, Archbishop Arundel excepted the parish priests when forbidding preaching without episcopal license. Finally Archbishop Nevill of York, 1465, set forth once more the leading points of the decrees which had been valid in England for nearly two centuries.[2]

Although the decrees provided for regularity of preaching, the problem of the average number of sermons preached in a year in the parishes of medieval England has not been solved. E. L. Cutts, in his work already cited, goes back to the Anglo-Saxon period for light upon this question, bringing together earlier instructions, for instance Aelfric's address to the clergy, c. 1030, and several decrees of synods and mandates of bishops from 1223 to 1395. This evidence, together with that relating to the Peckham Constitutions, Cutts interprets to mean that a sermon was preached in the parish churches on Sundays and holy days.[3] Cardinal Gasquet in his chapter on the *Parish Pulpit,* discusses the subject at considerable length, arriving at similar conclusions.[4] Regard-

[1] F. A. Gasquet, *Parish Life in Mediaeval England* (London: Methuen, 1907), p. 215.

[2] F. A. Gasquet, *ibid.,* pp. 215-217. E. L. Cutts, *Parish Priests and Their People* (London: S.P.C.K., 1914), pp. 216-223.

[3] Cutts, *ibid.,* pp. 214-216.

[4] Gasquet, *op. cit.,* chap. x. For Professor Coulton's refutation of

ing the injunctions of Archbishop Peckham, he points out that four sermons were necessary to cover the subjects of instruction mentioned in the Constitutions, and that the series of four being delivered four times, sixteen sermons in all were required for the fulfillment of this particular duty. Such a series was among the first books printed by Caxton in England. A most interesting distinction is made by Cardinal Gasquet between the " sermon " which was devoted to the proving or exposition of theological principles and the " instruction ", less formal in character, which was concerned with matters of faith and practice. At the present time a " sermon " may be of either kind. Perhaps the greater frequency of the latter than of the former type of discourse in the medieval parish church has led to a misunderstanding as to the actual number of sermons that were preached, if the word is used in a general sense. Owst believes that in all probability sermons were preached in cathedrals and abbey churches every Sunday. This is a more conservative estimate than that of Cardinal Gasquet who thinks that the sermon was heard in all parishes. Owst mentions the congregations gathered at preaching crosses in cemeteries connected with cathedral, convent or parish church. Preaching naves in friary churches later testify to congregations assembled there.[1]

On the other hand, if parochial duties had not often been neglected, it would have been unnecessary to promulgate the constitutions of Peckham to correct these evils. A like reforming zeal inspired Archbishop Thoresby of York, 1357, to issue the *Lay Folks' Catechism,* translated at the same time

Cardinal Gasquet's statements *vide* G. G. Coulton, *Medieval Studies* (London: Simkin—Kent, 1915), Appendix I, 1st series, 2nd edition, pp. 103-114.

[1] G. R. Owst, *Preaching in Medieval England* (Cambridge: Univ. Press, 1926), chap. v. For evidence showing that continuous Sunday preaching was exceptional in parish churches *vide* pp. 25-48, 235.

into English by John de Gaytrick, a monk of the Abbey of St. Mary's at York. The metrical form of the translation was intended to facilitate the memorizing of the teachings contained, by those who could not read. Modeled after the constitutions this little manual of religious faith and practice was widely disseminated.

Perhaps the best way to get a rough idea of the quality and quantity of medieval preaching in English is to depart entirely from the evidence of church decrees and official mandates, and to read over the list of books provided for the clergy in preparing sermons, and for laymen in practicing what had been preached. Cardinal Gasquet provides a bibliography of twenty-six works on clerical duty, instructions and sermons, and twenty more on religious instruction and preaching, some written in Latin, others in English.[1] The most complete list of such works in the vernacular is provided by J. E. Wells, who describes fifty-two compositions of all kinds, with the following introductory statement:

Necessity for making accessible and for disseminating the principal elements of Christian knowledge, for assisting to comprehension and practise of Christian conduct, and for directing to understanding of the services of the church and to due regard for them, led to production in Middle English of a number of writings ranging from volumes of elaborated composition to mere translation of the Pater Noster or mere statement of the names of the Seven Sins.[2]

Such an array of aids to instruction and preaching indicate the existence in medieval England of a demand which must have been the result of actual religious training undertaken by the clergy.

[1] Gasquet, *op. cit.*, pp. xiv, xv, xvii, xviii.

[2] J. E. Wells, *Manual of the Writings in Middle English* (New Haven: Yale Univ. Press, 1916), chap. vi. Works of Religious Information and Instruction and Aids to Church Services. *Vide* also two supplements, 1923.

Two great works of popular religious information and instruction selected from the Middle English group, which appeared shortly after 1300, were *Handlyng Synne* by Robert Mannyng of Brunne and *Ayenbite of Inwyt* (Remorse of Conscience). Both belong to a sequence of tracts originating in France, which will be described in a later section. Both were intended primarily for the common people. Robert Mannyng says that he wrote for this class, having in mind the games, feasts and alehouse gatherings where his rhymes might be welcome, shorn as they were of all subtlety, and extensively illustrated with timely stories.[1] The *Ayenbite of Inwyt* was written in the local dialect of Kent in order to secure a wider audience among the neighborhood group.[2]

Several other important works of religious instruction might be mentioned. One must suffice, namely *The Prymer,* or *Lay Folks' Prayer Book,* influential from the thirteenth century to the end of the Middle Ages. It was extremely common, one of the best known medieval books in England. Its use is proved by more than a dozen manuscripts in English, by twenty-nine printed editions between 1534 and 1547, and by the large number of wills in which it is mentioned. The *Prymer,* sometimes called the *Book of Hours,* contained the Hours of the Blessed Virgin, Seven Penitential Psalms, Fifteen Gradual Psalms, Litany, Office for the Dead, Commendations, etc.[3] According to the *Prymer* of the Salisbury Use, the Seven Deadly Sins are named as *pride, envie, wrathe, covetise, slouthe, glotenye, leccherie.* The form of confession of pride runs as follows: *I have sinned in pryde of herte, not lowly thankynge God of gyftes and connynge which he hath lent me. Also I have sinned in pryde of clotynge: in*

---

[1] Robert Mannyng, *Handlyng Synne* (E.E.T.S., O.S., 119, 123), verses 42-56.

[2] Dan Michel, *Ayenbite of Inwyt* (E.E.T.S., O.S., 23).

[3] Wordsworth and Littlehales, *Old Service Books of the English Church* (London: Methuen, 1904), chap. ix.

strength: in eloquence: in beaute: in proude words—Wherof I cry God mercy.[1] Not only in such explicit terms were the sins mentioned but the Penitential Psalms, wherever they appeared, reminded the reader or hearer of the duty of examining his conscience since each one was directed against a specific sin.[2]

All sides of the problem of religious education for the common man in the Middle Ages have by no means been viewed when the aspects of preaching and instruction through books of devotion have been considered. Preachers have been known to confront empty pews. Books of devotion have not always been well-thumbed. Much depends upon the average of attendance upon the services held and the observance of devotional offices within the place of worship on the part of the laity. Many services, which did not include preaching, were provided with some of the finest of the medieval hymns and other liturgical features from which the responsive worshipper may have learned much. To benefit by the opportunity offered, it was necessary to take advantage of it.

It seems to be generally conceded that public services on Sunday consisted of matins, mass and evensong. A daily mass in honor of the Virgin, the " Mary Mass ", or " Lady Mass ", was very generally celebrated in cathedrals, abbey, collegiate and parochial churches.[3] At Salisbury Cathedral the Lady Mass instituted by Bishop Poore in 1225, gave its name to the " Salve " chapel, a striking proof of the observance of this service.[4] Cardinal Gasquet gives evidence from

---

[1] Published in Maskell, *Monumenta Ritualia*, III, p. 293 *et seq.*

[2] *Vide Sarum Breviary*, II, 242 *et seq.*; Ps. vi, *contra iram*: xxxi, *contra superbiam*: xxxvii, *contra gulam*: l, *contra luxuriam*: ci, *contra avaritiam*: cxxix, *contra invidiam*: cxlii, *contra accidiam*. (The Vulgate numbering is given here.)

[3] J. E. Bridgett, *Our Lady's Dowry* (London: Burns & Oates, no date), 4th edition, pp. 155-158.

[4] C. Wordsworth, *Notes on Medieval Services* (London: Baker, 1898), p. 274.

fifteenth-century records of the celebration of a daily mass which, in his words, " was fairly attended by those whose duties permitted them to be present ".[1]

Whether the majority of the country folk availed themselves of the opportunity to attend church services on Sunday or week days is a subject of controversy.   As to Sunday worship, the famous lines from *Piers Plowman* which are quoted below, if read in their context, indicate rather a " counsel of perfection " than a description of actual facts.

219   " For holy church hoteth alle manere puple,
220   Under obedience to bee, and buxum to the lawe,

223   Lewede men to labore, lordes to honte,

227   And upon Sonedays to cesse, Godes seruyce to huyre,
228   Both matyns and messe, and after mete in churches
229   To huyre here eve-song, euery man ouhte." [2]

Yet *Piers Plowman* is so closely associated with peasant life that its aspirations in any field may not be ignored.   Second only to *Canterbury Tales* as a literary product of the Middle English period, the poem must have exerted a devotional influence comparable to that of the leading works written expressly for religious and didactic purposes.   " In reality, it represents nothing more nor less than the quintessence of English medieval preaching gathered up into a single metrical piece of unusual charm and vivacity." [3]

Light is thrown upon the problem of medieval church attendance by the fact that Catholicism has always emphasized the necessity of this practice as a matter of discipline.   Certain regulations, for example, the Friday fast, the annual communion at Easter, the annual confession of sins, attendance at obligatory feasts and attendance at mass on Sunday, go back

[1] F. A. Gasquet, *op. cit.*, p. 144.
[2] Passus X, C–Text (E.E.T.S., 54), p. 170.
[3] Owst, *op. cit.*, p. 295.

for centuries. The requirement of attendance at weekly mass dates from the days of the Roman Empire.[1] In the Middle Ages, as Villien makes clear, the obligation to attend mass meant attendance in the church of the parish in which the individual resided. Decrees restricting the worshipper to a particular parish or forbidding the reception of strangers are indicative of the practice in general. The commands of the Council of Rouen, 1235, and Trier, 1238, are representative of continental legislation, while the Statutes of the Synod of Chichester, 1246, and the Council of Oxford, 1287, manifest the importance attached to church attendance in thirteenth-century England.[2]

The architectural features of the church edifice itself have been used by Owst to demonstrate the presence of congregations in friary churches, that is, the " preaching naves," to which attention has already been directed. The very existence of the church building as well as its architectural form, is presumptive evidence of the activities which were carried on within its walls. Among these preaching must be included, whether frequent or infrequent, whether heard by few or many. The actual number of churches existing in England in the Middle Ages, may be estimated roughly from the studies which have been made in English church dedications. Those erected before the Reformation, according to the statistics offered by Frances Arnold-Foster, number 10.-569.[3] It would seem incredible that they were largely unattended and their services neglected. Substantial contributions, popular enthusiasm, communal pride, the weight of tradition and convention, go into the making of a church

---

[1] A. Villien, *Histoire des Commandements de l'Église* (Paris: Lecoffre, 1909), p. 26.

[2] Villien, *ibid.*, pp. 42-46.

[3] *Studies in Church Dedications* (London: Skeffington & Son, 1899), vol. iii.

building and are important factors in its support.   When
these were reinforced by ecclesiastical authority imposed upon
all classes in the community, it may be assumed that the
public services of the church summoned to its doors the bulk
of the population, and of course the peasantry among them.

As in England, so in France and other countries of western
Europe, decrees of councils, books of sermons, manuals of
instruction, religious and devotional works provided for the
laity, and the very existence of hundreds of church buildings
offer evidence which is helpful toward an understanding of
the religious life of persons outside the more highly educated
classes.   Since the field is too large for adequate treatment
here and the chief emphasis of this study has been placed upon
conditions in England, the continental devotional and instruc-
tional literature only will be mentioned and very briefly.
Brunet has included in his catalogue of books printed in the
French language before 1500, sixty-five titles of works on
moral and religious subjects.   In his great *Manuel du
Libraire,* a large space in volume V is devoted to the editions
of the *Heures.*[1]   Bohatta's comprehensive bibliography of
the *Heures* names 1479 different editions.[2]   Naturally the
familiar categories of sins and virtues are much in evidence in
this literature.   The works of Étienne de Bourbon and of
Perrault, which will be described later, must not be overlooked
as additional testimony pointing to the prevalence of religious
instruction for the lower classes, as the popularity of the
vernacular translations of Perrault's manual bears witness.
Still, the evidence of all kinds is too meager for a complete
reconstruction of the religion of the peasant on this ground
alone.

France whose soil is sacred with the memories of saints like

[1] G. Brunet, *La France littéraire au XVe Siècle* (Paris: Franck, 1865).
G. Brunet, *Manuel du Libraire* (Paris: Didot, 1861).

[2] H. Bohatta, *Bibliographie der Livres d'Heures des XV. und XVI.
Jahrhunderts* (Wien: Gilhofer & Ranschburg, 1924).

Martin, Bernard and Louis, and whose literature abounds in records of every phase of religious experience, should have been the last place in Europe to neglect the lowlier members of the household of faith.   Yet the impression of rustic religion in the early thirteenth century which is conveyed by Luchaire is exceedingly gloomy.   Testimony to the contrary is scant but the impression may be somewhat relieved by contemplating the religious faith of two uneducated French women, the mother of François Villon, and Joan of Arc. Though they lived at a later period than that described by Luchaire it is probable that conditions were similar in both centuries although the influence of the friars must not be overlooked.   For François' mother there remains that most naive and appealing expression of devotion to which Villon himself gave poetic form.[1]   For Joan, her recorded statements made during her trial at Rouen, interpreted simply as a revelation of the mind of a peasant girl, with due allowance for the unusual circumstances and for instructions which she may have received, contain a creed which has been found conformable to the strictest demands of orthodoxy.   Peasant saints in the Middle Ages may be extremely rare, as Professor Coulton tells us, but this particular saint, so far as her simple piety and unshaken faith are concerned, may conceivably be representative of the peasant attitude.   However one interprets Joan's " voices " at least this point seems clear. She knew a great deal about certain saints.   So did other people of very restricted intellectual horizon throughout medieval Europe.   " Further down in the social scale, legends furnished the peasant with recreation, when read to him or recited to him—perhaps by some of the vagabonds who were his mental superiors and his social equals ; and they gave him new materials for fireside tales." [2]   The existence of

[1] Villon, *Ballade pour prier Nostre Dame*; *Oeuvres*, edited by A. Longnon (Paris: Champion, 1914), p. 40.

[2] G. H. Gerould, *Saints' Legends*, pp. 14-15.

legends of the saints as well as instructions in the vernacular demonstrate the probability at least that the peasant shared, perhaps very largely, the point of view on religious matters familiar to other social groups.   It is, moreover, a type of evidence equally significant in all parts of Christendom and closely related to the evidence from manuals of instruction and of popular devotion.

This very brief sketch of the possibilities for a study of peasant religion would not be complete without mention of the German sources other than legends of saints.   Berthold of Regensburg and his sermons will be cited elsewhere.   One might expand the topic of popular preaching in the vernacular, especially after 1215, and of homiletic guides, of which the *Buch der Rügen* written in Latin and German is a fair illustration.[1]   Humbert of Romans, a Dominican leader, wrote another well-known work on the art of preaching.   Although a Burgundian, he exerted a great influence in Germany.   So too, did Guibert of Nogent, who composed a preacher's manual, and Alan of Lille (d. 1202?), whose *Summa* was an important homiletic guide.   All three flourished in the late twelfth and thirteenth centuries.[2]

One might bring forward also the poetry of rustic life, for example, the poem of Wernher der Gärtner, *Meier Helmbrecht,* which portrays in the character of the elder Helmbrecht, a peasant of noble ideals with a strong sense of the dignity of toil.   Again, one might cite the religious folk poetry to which the Minnesänger made substantial contributions; or the evidence of Thomas of Cantimpré who describes the life of the peasant in the Netherlands, illustrating the attendance of the peasants upon mass, their penance, fasting, prayer and almsgiving.[3]

[1] E. Michael, *Geschichte des deutschen Volkes*, II, 102.

[2] E. Michael, *ibid.*, pp. 100-102.

[3] A. Kaufman, " Thomas von Chantimpré über das Bürger- und Bauerleben seiner Zeit ", *Zeitschrift f. deutsche Kulturgeschichte*, N.F. 3 (1893), 299-301.

Such are the lines of inquiry suggested by the question of the actual participation of the uneducated classes during the Middle Ages in the rites of their religion, and the amount and nature of contemporary religious instruction. The following chapters will be devoted to the intensive study of ethical ideals appearing in the Latin hymns of medieval England and the correspondence of these ideals with related contemporary forms of ethical expression.

CHAPTER I

THE ENGLISH COLLECTIONS

THE chief Latin hymns used in medieval England are recorded in the principal liturgies which prevailed in England during the Middle Ages, namely, the rites of the bishoprics of Sarum, York, Hereford, Lincoln and Bangor. Of these the liturgy of Sarum or *Use of Sarum,* as it is called, ranked first in importance. Monastic orders, also, possessed their distinctive rites which included hymns not appearing in the liturgies mentioned above. The nucleus of all the collections, whether episcopal or monastic, is identical. It is the purpose of this chapter to trace the historical growth and development, first, of the group of hymns common to all the English liturgies, and second, of the variable group which forms the characteristic element in any liturgy studied by itself. The second part of the chapter will be devoted to the four groups of hymns which have been selected as the most representative in medieval England, i. e., the Sarum hymns, the York hymns, the Hereford hymns and a small number selected from monastic rites. In addition to these four groups other pieces have been chosen from two source collections which were used in compiling the liturgies of Sarum, York and Hereford, but not included in them. The nature and importance of both source collections will be explained later.

The word *hymn* is used in two senses in Latin hymnology. It means either *hymn* or *sequence,* the exact definitions of which should be expanded at this point. Ambrose, his contemporaries and his imitators, composed hymns in metrical stanzas employing chiefly the iambic tetrameter, which set the fashion for several centuries.   In the ninth century the *sequence* appeared, first in the form of rythmical prose, then in the form of rhymed meters.   The *hymn* in the former sense may be defined as " metrical poetry consecrated to the celebration of Christian truths and religious events." [1]   Christian services early included such hymns and St. Benedict himself adopted them for monastic use, as his Rule indicates. Hymns of this kind are found in the breviaries of the various medieval liturgies.

The general term hymn may also indicate a *sequence* (*sequentia*), or *prose* (*prosa*) as it was named in France.   Fundamentally they are similar, both being additions to the alleluia of the mass.   W. H. Frere and others regard the sequence as a trope, or liturgical interpolation added to a musical part of the service.[2]   F. J. E. Raby, on the other hand, warns against classing the sequence as a trope, a term which he believes must be restricted to additions made to the Introit, Kyrie or Gloria or similar features of the liturgy.[3] The fact remains, however, that the English word *troper* or *tropary* (*troparium*), means a service book containing sequences as well as other tropes.   In the same way, the English words *hymner* and *hymnary* (*hymnarium*) denote a service book containing hymns.   The undoubted preference on the part of students of Latin hymnology for the name sequence to indicate the new type of hymn which originated in the ninth century, has determined its use in this study.

The most distinguishing feature of the sequence is its evolution within the mass.   Hence sequences are found in the missal, while hymns are found in the breviary.   Procession-

---

[1] H. Leclercq in *Dictionnaire d'Archéologie chrétienne et de Liturgie*; Hymnes, VI, Hymnographie dans l'Eglise latine.

[2] W. H. Frere, *The Winchester Troper* (London: Harrison, 1894), Henry Bradshaw Soc. Pub., vol. viii, Introduction, p. viii *et seq.*

[3] F. J. E. Raby, *History of Christian-Latin Poetry* (Oxford: Clarendon Press, 1927), p. 219.

als may be of either type, and are found in the processional, or service book devoted to processional ceremonies. Whenever it becomes necessary to differentiate between the hymn and sequence in the following pages the technical meaning will be made clear. In general the word hymn will be employed to include both.

In studying the Use of Sarum or any other medieval liturgy a question naturally arises as to the source of the hymns in the breviary and of the sequences in the missal. The question can be answered in the case of the breviary by tracing the origin and the evolution of the traditional cycle of hymns which had been handed down from the early medieval centuries. In the case of the missal the problem of sources is more perplexing but still capable of solution, at least in part.

The Benedictine Rule, as noted above, contains directions for the singing of hymns in the services of the canonical hours but specific hymns are not mentioned. Caesarius of Arles and his successor Aurelian, who were contemporaries of St. Benedict, indicate in their monastic Rules the actual hymns which were used.[1] These Rules, together with a small group of hymnals of the seventh to the ninth centuries, furnish the full list of the primitive cycle of hymns. It includes thirty-five hymns in two groups, those for Easter and those for the rest of the year. St. Augustine, the Benedictine missionary to Kent, brought the cycle to England.[2]

Ever since the publication of Father Blume's work upon the subject of the Benedictine hymnal, it has been frequently

[1] A. S. Walpole, *Early Latin Hymns* (Cambridge: University Press, 1922), Introduction, p. xi *et seq.*

[2] C. Blume, *Der Cursus S. Benedicti Nursini und die liturgischen Hymnen des 6.-9. Jahrhunderts* (Leipzig: Reisland, 1908), p. 48 *et seq.* For a brief discussion of the primitive cycle and the list of hymns which it includes *vide*, W. H. Frere, *Hymns Ancient and Modern* (London: Clowes and Sons, 1909), Historical Edition, Introduction, pp. xiv-xv. A. S. Walpole, *op. cit.*, also prints the list but gives thirty-six hymns. Introduction, pp. xii-xiv.

asserted that the primitive cycle was overturned during the ninth century by an Anglo-Irish cycle which superseded it. Blume reconstructed the early cycle by piecing together two parts of one manuscript preserved respectively in St. Paul's monastery in Carinthia and at Karlsruhe.[1] In a full discussion of Blume's findings Raby presents a somewhat different theory, namely, that the hymns of the Anglo-Irish cycle were not superimposed from the north but that they represent a new stage in the development of the old Benedictine hymnal.[2] Whatever the origin of the ninth-century cycle may prove to be, upon further investigation, the list of hymns in the cycle remains the same. They are the nucleus of later medieval hymn collections with additional compositions provided to celebrate the various festivals of the liturgical seasons and the feast days of saints.[3] Three groups of hymns instead of two, characterize the new cycle, corresponding to the three divisions of the liturgy, hymns for the Proper of the Season, those for the Common of Saints, and those for the Proper of Saints. Later additions to the hymnal were made in accordance with these lines of division.[4]

The *Bosworth Psalter,* a tenth-century psalter of Canterbury, includes a complete cycle of hymns used in England.[5] There is practically no difference between the list of Bosworth hymns and that of the ninth-century cycle except for certain

[1] W. H. Frere, *op. cit.,* Introduction, p. xvi. Frere refers to Blume's work just cited.

[2] Raby, *op. cit.,* pp. 36-40.

[3] Walpole's work cited above is an intensive study of the two series, containing 130 hymns, under the titles *The Old Hymnal* and *The Later Hymnal.*

[4] Frere, in his introduction cited above prints the list of hymns in the Anglo-Irish cycle, grouping them in accordance with the liturgical divisions, p. xvi.

[5] F. A. Gasquet and E. Bishop, *The Bosworth Psalter* (London: Bell, 1908), pp. 12, 13.

additions which appear, in turn, in eleventh-century collections. The Sarum collection is essentially the same, many hymns being duplicated also in the liturgies of York and Hereford.

Throughout medieval Christendom of the eleventh century, there was little variety in the traditional list of hymns which were sung in different localities. A general uniformity in the chief festivals and saints' days which were determined by Roman models, resulted in the use of similar hymns. This was particularly the case with the groups of hymns for the Proper of the Season and the Common of Saints. With the coming of the twelfth century a great difference is perceptible due to the appearance of local cults which made necessary the introduction of many new hymns for the praises of saints in local calendars. English liturgies, however, were exceptional in this respect, that fewer hymns were introduced for this purpose and for later medieval feasts.[1]

The sequences of the missal differ greatly from the hymns of the breviary in several respects. There is, for instance, a much smaller proportion of sequences common to all missals than of hymns common to all breviaries, because the lists lack a single tradition. Several monastic centers produced sequences at about the same period, among them, St. Gall, where Notker was the leading composer, and Limoges, representative of French genius. The French school developed its greatest influence later than the German school, largely through the talents of Adam of St. Victor.[2] Variety in the lists of sequences due to selections made from rival schools is increased by the demands of local cults and also by the need for special compositions to ornament the services of late medieval feasts such as the feasts of the Virgin.

When the collections of hymns and sequences are under-

[1] W. H. Frere, *op. cit.*, Introduction, p. xxiv.
[2] W. H. Frere, *The Winchester Troper*, pp. xii-xiii.

stood in the light of their history, the problem of chronology as well as that of sources is partially solved.   Exact chronology is impossible in the study of medieval hymns of all kinds because the dates and authors of most of them are unknown. It is possible however, to determine approximate dates for many of them by referring to the earliest manuscripts in which they appear, particularly the manuscripts of hymnaries and troparies which mark definite stages in the evolution of liturgical poetry.   Thus the hymns for the hour services constitute the most ancient group and the pieces composed for fifteenth-century feasts the latest group in the medieval centuries.   While the chronology cannot be worked out in every detail, at least three large groups of compositions can be formed, corresponding to three periods, namely, hymns first used in the fourth to the eighth centuries, in the ninth to the twelfth centuries and in the thirteenth to the fifteenth centuries.

The importance of the Sarum liturgy in the English medieval church is indicated by the literature which exists upon the subject, especially its origin and characteristic forms.   The Use of Sarum, it appears, was established by Bishop Osmund, one of those Norman administrators and clerics who accompanied William the Conqueror to England.   Under William, Osmund held the office of chancellor.[1]   He exchanged political for ecclesiastical honors when he became Bishop of Sarum, 1078, a position which he held until his death in 1099.[2]   Among the important tasks which he accomplished during this period, was the revision of the liturgy, made necessary by the varieties of ritual which were growing up in the different localities of England.   A group of scholars was

[1] W. H. Rich-Jones, *Register of St. Osmund*, Rolls Series, vol. 78(2), Introduction, p. xxiii.   *Sarum Charters and Documents*, Rolls Series, vol. 97, p. 373.

[2] William of Malmesbury, *Gesta Pontificum*, Rolls Series, vol. 52, pp. 183-184.

accordingly assembled at Sarum, the library enlarged by the accession and transcribing of books, and liturgical studies undertaken which gave rise to the Sarum rites.[1] Based on Gregorian sources, the revised liturgy unified the Anglo-Saxon and Norman practices of the time.[2] It took definite form in the *Ordinal* or *Consuetudinary* which was thereafter associated with the name of Osmund.[3] The Use of Sarum attained great popularity and was adopted widely throughout Britain and particularly southern England.[4]

Osmund's liturgical studies resulted in the gradual preparation of service books including all parts of the ritual. That they were extensively employed is proved not only by many references dating from medieval times but by the large number of printed editions which appeared in the late fifteenth and sixteenth centuries, especially of the breviary and missal.[5] Copies of these, as well as of the *antiphonale, diurnale, legenda, ordinale* or *pica, directorium sacerdotum, psalterium cum hymnis, hymni cum notis,* etc., remain to us. It is impossible, however, to estimate the popularity or diffusion of

[1] W. H. Rich-Jones, *op. cit.*, Rolls Series, vol. 78(1), Introduction, p. xiv; vol. 78(2), Introduction, p. xxix *et seq.*, p. 88. Wilkins, *Concilia*, I, 715. Peter of Blois, *Epistula* 133, (PL, ccvii, 595-596). William of Malmesbury, *op. cit.*, pp. 183-184.

[2] H. B. Swete, *Church Services and Service Books* (London: S.P.C.K., 1896), p. 15.

[3] "He (Osmund) also composed an *Ordinal* or *Consuetudinarium*, comprising directions and rubrics for the uniform celebration of the Holy Sacrifice, the Divine Office, and the administration of the Sacraments." R. Stanton, *Menology of England and Wales* (London: Burns and Oates, 1892), p. 584.

[4] For a more detailed account of the origin and diffusion of the Sarum Use, *vide* R. Messenger, "Hymns and Sequences of the Sarum Use", *Transactions and Proceedings of the Amer. Philological Ass.*, 59 (1928), 99-129.

[5] For a list of the early editions of the breviary, *vide* Procter and Wordsworth, *Breviarium*, Appendix II. A list of early editions of the missal can be found in Dickinson, *Missal*, Preface, pp. lvi-lxxii.

any English medieval ritual by the number of manuscripts or early printed editions now extant. The activities of the Reformation party brought about their all but total destruction, as the episcopal injunctions of that day bear witness.[1] The actual copies of manuscripts or books now available must be multiplied many times over to afford an idea of the number in the hands of clergy and laymen in the medieval period.

Interest in the subject of ancient English liturgies was stimulated in the middle of the nineteenth century by the Oxford Movement, in connection with which, or as a result of which, so many suggestive lines of scholarly investigation were indicated. In the field of Latin hymnology alone, the names of Neale and Caswall are familiar not only to every student of the subject, but to thousands who have been inspired by their translations of medieval hymns.

The Latin texts of the Sarum hymns are found not only in the breviary and missal but in special service books, namely, *psalterium, hymni Sarum cum notis, processionale,* and also in the *expositio hymnorum et sequentiarum* which sometimes appears in two parts. The last, however, is not strictly speaking a service book but a school book for religious and grammatical instruction. Between the lines of the hymn or sequence is written an *expositio* or paraphrase explaining the thought and pointing out the construction of the sentence. The lists of hymns made from the *psalterium,* the *hymni Sarum* and the *expositio hymnorum* are practically identical. Again, the lists of hymns and sequences derived from the above are essentially the same as those derived from the breviary and missal, allowing for the duplication of some twenty of the missal sequences in the breviary. A short additional list appears in the Sarum processional. We have therefore, a total of 231 poems of which 119 appear in the breviary, 101 in the missal and the remaining 11 in the pro-

---

[1] W. H. Frere and W. M. Kennedy, *Visitation Articles and Injunctions* (London: Longmans, Green & Co., 1910), vol. iii, *passim.*

cessional which also contains ten duplicated from the breviary or missal.[1]

The general history of the traditional cycle of Latin hymns and its development has been indicated already. It now remains to examine more closely the lists of hymns and sequences found in manuscripts extant in eleventh-century England in order to discover the material actually available for the liturgists of Osmund's time. The hymns and sequences which were added in the period from the eleventh to the sixteenth century must also be accounted for as far as possible.

Present knowledge as to the hymn collections of eleventh-century England is based upon five manuscripts of *hymnaria* namely, the *Durham Hymnary,* two Cottonian manuscripts of hymnaries, a *collectarium* or breviary without the Psalter, and a complete hymnary accompanying a psalter written soon after 1064.[2] The first of these which is preserved in the Library of the Dean and Chapter at Durham, has received the name of *Durham Hymnarium,* although Joseph Stevenson who edited it for the Surtees Society in 1851 considered it to be of southern English origin, perhaps written at Winchester.[3] If true, the point is significant because of the position held by Winchester as a center of interest in church music. Stevenson's edition of the collection is made more valuable by the inclusion of a few hymns from the eleventh-century Cottonian manuscripts, making a total of 153 hymns. In this way, a collection largely representative of the hymns used by the Anglo-Saxon church was obtained.[4] The Sarum

[1] It is impossible to give exact numbers because parts of hymns were used as separate units. These figures do not include parts.

[2] *Durham Hymnarium,* MS Library of the Dean and Chapter, Durham. Cottonian MS, Julius A. vi. Cottonian MS, Vespasian D. xii. Harleian MS, 2961: *Collectarium.* Corpus Christi College, Cambridge MS, 391: *Psalter.*

[3] J. Stevenson, *Latin Hymns of the Anglo-Saxon Church*, Preface, p. viii.

[4] Stevenson, *ibid.,* Preface, p. x.

breviary contains 79 hymns which are found in this collection. The large extent to which the collection is represented in other medieval liturgies may be observed by examining the list of hymns printed by Julian.[1]　For this reason all the hymns published by Stevenson whether or not they appear in the hymnals of Sarum, York or Hereford have been included in the total number used in this study.

There are still thirty hymns to be accounted for in the Sarum breviary.　Most of them have been dated approximately by the editors of the larger Latin hymn collections or by other students of medieval hymnology on the basis of their appearance in manuscripts, the dates of which are known. Thus 88 belong to the period before 1100, three to the twelfth century, four to the thirteenth century, four to the fourteenth century, nine to the fifteenth century, five to the sixteenth century, while six are undated.　The hymns which appear after 1100 are, for the most part, those provided for the later feasts and for the Proper of Saints.　An interesting correspondence is observable between the results of analyzing the Sarum collection from the point of view of its history and the point of view of its sources.　While this was only to be expected it does emphasize the larger divisions of the subject matter in the liturgical hymns, the evolution of the collections and their chronology.

Turning to the sequences of the Sarum missal, we find certain important sources to be extant, notably the *Winchester Troper*.　Winchester, already mentioned as a center of interest in church music, and the possible place of origin of the *Durham Hymnary,* exerted an influence in England like that of Bangor in Ireland, or St. Gall in central Europe. There are two manuscripts of the Winchester Troper in existence, one, called the *Tropary of Ethelred* because it was

---

[1] J. Julian, *Dictionary of Hymnology* (London: Murray, 1908), p. 172 *et seq.*

written during the reign of Ethelred between 979 and 1016; the other, the *Winchester Troper,* written some fifty years later.[1]　There are thirty-one Winchester sequences in the Sarum missal.

As in the case of the hymn sources published in Stevenson's *Latin Hymns of the Anglo-Saxon Church,* the *Winchester Troper* constituted an important element in English liturgies.　The connection may be traced from Julian's list of sequences.[2]　Therefore, all the sequences in the Winchester collection irrespective of their appearance in the rites of Sarum, York or Hereford have been included in this study.

In order to discover whether any of the remaining sequences antedate 1100 the collections related to the Winchester Troper must be sought.　It seems probable that the actual source of the Troper was in Fleury-sur-Loire whence had come, via Abingdon, the Benedictine monks who transcribed the *Tropary of Ethelred.*[3]　Important connections therefore, existed between Winchester and Fleury-sur-Loire, which in turn, seems to have been influenced by Limoges.　This is attested by the edition of Limoges sequences made by Dreves in the seventh volume of the *Analecta Hymnica Medii Aevi.*　Twenty sequences appear both in the Limoges and the Winchester collections, and also in the Sarum missal.　To these must be added five more Limoges sequences antedating 1100, as well as nine more assigned to the same period by various editors.　Therefore, forty-five

---

[1] The two manuscripts are Bodleian 775 and Corpus Christi College, Cambridge, 473.　The Winchester sequences have been edited as follows: *The Tropary of Ethelred,* Surtees Soc. Pub., vol. 60, Appendix to the *York Missal,* edited by W. G. Henderson.　The *Winchester Troper,* Henry Bradshaw Soc. Pub., vol. viii, edited by W. H. Frere.

[2] J. Julian, *Dictionary of Hymnology,* p. 1043 *et seq.*

[3] W. H. Frere, *Winchester Troper,* p. xxix.　H. M. Bannister, *Anal. Hymn.,* XL, p. 9.

sequences are accounted for in the early group. Light is shed upon the problem of dating the remaining sequences by the so-called Lord Crawford manuscript of the Sarum missal, which may be dated between 1150 and 1319.[1] It contains twelve sequences not in the early group but probably known before 1300. With these may be placed fifteen others, according to leading editors of Latin hymns, making twenty-seven in all for the second group. Similarly the twenty-eight remaining sequences may be assigned to later centuries on the authority of the best known students of medieval hymnology. This has been done as follows: ten to the fourteenth century, eight to the fifteenth century, nine to the sixteenth century while one is undated. The Sarum sequences therefore, fall into three large divisions. The first group, almost one-half of the entire number, antedates 1100. The second group, about one-fourth, belongs to the period between 1100 and 1319. The third group, about one-fourth, must be associated with the fourteenth, fifteenth and sixteenth centuries.

The eleven pieces from the Sarum processional which do not appear in the breviary or missal may be divided into two groups, of which seven belong to the period before 1100 and the other four after the thirteenth century.

The history of York and its importance in the ecclesiastical affairs of medieval England is too familiar to need full discussion here. Even from the days of the Roman occupation traditions of the Christian faith linger in the story of the district. Paulinus, in the generation following Augustine's mission to Kent, established Christianity in the northern kingdom of Northumbria and became its first bishop.[2] The centuries succeeding saw the rise to national importance of a

---

[1] *Sarum Missal*, edited by J. W. Legg (Oxford: Clarendon Press, 1916), Preface, p. vi.

[2] Bede, *Historia Ecclesiastica*, ii, 9.

diocese which rivalled that of Canterbury. Indeed, the struggles of the great primates of York and of Canterbury for the chief power in England were not settled until the pontificate of Innocent VI (1352-62), when they were ended by an agreement which gave them almost equal prestige.[1]

The extensive territorial limits of the diocese constituted an additional factor of great importance. At first identical with the boundaries of Northumbria, the diocese later included the shire of York—the largest in England—and Nottingham as well. It contained 541 parishes and numerous religious houses, notably of the Benedictines and Cistercians. The prominence of York in the field of learning was unquestioned. Names like those of Archbishop Egbert and of Alcuin suffice to remind the student of a reputation which had passed beyond England to the educational centers of the continent. A galaxy of northern saints, Aidan, Chad, Cuthbert, John of Beverley, William of York, enriched the traditions of the region. Nor were reformers lacking. It was Archbishop John de Thoresby (1352-73), who enforced in the north of England the policies of Archbishop Peckham of Canterbury which were effective in the south.

That uniformity of observance which the Use of Sarum had secured in the southern and central districts, found occasional favor, it is true, in the northern diocese but the local usage was too strong to be displaced. It is probable that Alcuin himself inspired the introduction of the Roman rite of the eighth century which was put into practice by Archbishop Eanbald II.[2] The resemblance between the two rituals of Sarum and York is very great, especially as regards their hymnology. The reasons for this have already

[1] G. Ornsby, *York: Diocesan Histories* (London: S.P.C.K., no date), p. 168.

[2] Alcuin, *Epist.*, lvi, lxv (PL, c. 224, 254). *Vide* also *Lay Folks Mass Book*, E.E.T.S., O.S., 71, p. 352.

been explained in the discussion of the history and sources of the Latin hymns used in England.   There are, it is true, a larger number of hymns and sequences in the York collection than in the Sarum but the great majority are identical.   For the present purpose the rites of Sarum and of York may be regarded as complementary, influential over most of England.   In fact the psalters and hymnals of Sarum and York were often printed together.[1]

Manuscripts and printed editions of the York rites are relatively rare.   There are only five early printed editions of the York missal known as contrasted with sixty-seven editions of the Sarum missal.[2]   A collation of seven manuscripts and five printed editions forms the basis of the modern edition of the York breviary in the Surtees Society Publications.[3]   One printed hymnal of 1517 exists.[4]   Lest this be interpreted as an indication of great inferiority of influence to the Sarum Use, it should be recalled that Archbishop Edmund Grindal, who was appointed to the See of York by Queen Elizabeth in 1570, in his enthusiasm for the new order required the absolute destruction of the old service books.[5]

These books were of course the repositories of the York hymns and sequences, the importance of which is attested by the separate edition of the hymnal and the combined editions of psalter and hymns either alone or with the Sarum hymns. In 1850 a modern edition of Sarum hymns appeared containing also a selection from the York and Hereford hymnals, comprising a total of 157 hymns.[6]   Approximately ninety-

[1] *Vide* Appendix to the *York Missal*, Surtees Soc. Pub., vol. 60.

[2] W. H. J. Weale, *Catalogus Missalium*, edited by H. Bohatta (London: Quaritch, 1928).

[3] *Vide* appendix to the *York Missal*, Sur. Soc. Pub., vol. 60.

[4] *York Missal, op. cit.*

[5] W. H. Frere, *Visitation Articles and Injunctions*, III, pp. 255, 285. Ornsby, *York*, p. 348.

[6] *Hymnale*, edited by Wilson and Stubbs (Littlemore: Masson, 1850).

seven hymns appear in both the York and Sarum breviaries
and sixty-five sequences are duplicated in the corresponding
missals.

The diocese of Hereford is located on the eastern border
of South Wales. Although its importance as a center of
Christianity may be traced to the sixth century, its ecclesiastical history dates from the close of the seventh century
when Bishop Putta became the head of the diocese in 676.[1]
Its early political prominence is indicated by the fact that the
town of Hereford was the ancient capital of the kingdom of
Mercia. In the century following the formation of the
diocese under Putta, Ethelbert, king of East Anglia, was
treacherously murdered in the palace of Offa, king of Mercia.
His tragic fate was the first of a series of events which raised
Hereford to the first rank as a place of pilgrimage in England. The cathedral, formerly dedicated to the Virgin, became the church of St. Mary and St. Ethelbert. The royal
saint, whose story will be discussed in another connection,
knew no rivals in the diocese until the growth of the cult of
St. Thomas of Hereford, some centuries later.

Doubtless King Offa did not foresee the increased prestige
for Hereford which was to result from his violation of the
laws of hospitality, but there can be no question that he
knowingly asserted the independence of the Mercian church
when he petitioned for an archbishopric of Lichfield in 786.
The ascendancy of Lichfield was temporary, however, for
Canterbury regained her control in Mercia after Offa's
death.[2]

Hereford took a prominent part in the political as well as
the ecclesiastical affairs of medieval England. In the civil

[1] A. H. Fisher, *Cathedral Church of Hereford* (London: Bell, 1898),
p. 90. Bede, *Historia Ecclesiastica*, iv, 12. W. Bright, *Chapters of Early
English Church History* (Oxford: Clarendon Press, 1888), pp. 273, 319.

[2] William of Malmesbury, *Gesta Regum*, i, 4, 87.

war between Stephen and Matilda the diocese threw its influence on Stephen's side.[1]   When the controversy arose between Henry II and Becket, Bishop Robert of Maledon attempted to reconcile the King and Archbishop.   That Becket
was later venerated in Hereford is indicated by the representation of the Archbishop in the cathedral in mural painting
and stained glass, by another Becket window in a neighboring
parish church, and by the continued recognition of the festival of the Translation of St. Thomas of Canterbury.   All
these marks of honor were prohibited by Henry VIII, yet this
much survived of what may have been more numerous evidences of Becket's influence.   The crusading ventures of
King Richard appealed to the men of Hereford, but the cause
of Edward II was repudiated.   Bishop Adam Orleton supported his deposition.   Lollardism was active in Hereford,
due to the influence of Sir John Oldcastle, known as Lord
Cobham, who protected the followers of Wycliffe.[2]

Among the bishops who occupied the See of Hereford,
Thomas de Cantelupe (b. 1220) was the most important.
His participation in public affairs and his chancellorship
under Henry III before his appointment as bishop are comparable to the incidents of Osmund's career.   Like Osmund
he too was canonized.   Indeed his fame as a local saint out-
stripped that of the Bishop of Salisbury and in Hereford was
second only to the prestige of St. Ethelbert.

This very brief sketch of the outstanding points in the
history of Hereford diocese may yield some explanation of
the fact that the Use of Hereford, among the various rituals
which persisted until Reformation times, ranks next to those
of Sarum and York in its vitality and the extent to which it
was adopted.   Although the neighboring dioceses of St.

---

[1] H. W. Phillott, *Hereford: Diocesan Histories* (London: S.P.C.K.,
1888), pp. 40-41.

[2] Phillott, *ibid.*, pp. 45-47, 48, 49, 103-104, 122.

David's and of Lichfield favored the Sarum Use, Hereford remained unaffected.[1] The origin of the Use of Hereford cannot be determined but it dates from an early period.[2] Putta, the first bishop, was skilled in church music, for he instructed others in the art which he had acquired from scholars of the period of Gregory the Great.[3] The Use of Hereford varies from the other great liturgies and yet is harmonious with them, especially with that of Sarum.[4]

One printed edition of the Hereford missal of the year 1502 [5] is extant, and one printed Hereford breviary of 1505. The modern edition of the breviary by Frere and Brown is a revision of the edition of 1505 in the light of five manuscripts. One is a complete thirteenth-century breviary but the other four contain portions only.[6] The hymns of the breviary are also found in an antiphonary of 1265, another rare Hereford service book.[7]

A comparison of the lists of hymns in the Hereford breviary and sequences in the Hereford missal with the corresponding Sarum lists reveals the same similarity that was found in the comparison between York and Sarum. As a matter of fact the breviary hymns are not even printed in full in the edition of Frere and Brown when they are identical with those of Sarum. This occurs in some 103 instances. The hymns and sequences common to all three liturgies constitute a very large proportion of the entire number—a circumstance most favorable to their use in the interpretation

[1] W. Maskell, *Ancient Liturgy of the Church of England,* 3rd edition, (Oxford: Clarendon Press, 1882), p. lxv.

[2] W. Maskell, *ibid.,* p. lxv.

[3] Phillott, *op. cit.,* p. 9.

[4] Maskell, *op. cit.,* p. lxxi. Phillott, *op. cit.,* pp. 65-66.

[5] Weale, *Catalogus Missalium.*

[6] *Hereford Breviary,* Henry Bradshaw Soc. Pub., vol. 26, Preface.

[7] Phillott, *op. cit.,* pp. 67-68.

of widespread religious ideas. The variable portion of the three collections is no less interesting. It illustrates the tendency towards differentiation which was characteristic of the liturgical hymns and sequences after the twelfth century. Local saints already mentioned, for instance, occupy an important position in the lists. The variety, however, consists in the number of different compositions for similar purposes and not so much in the ideas which are expressed. For example, several different pieces in different liturgies may be written for the same feast or different local saints may be praised in similar terms.

James Mearns in *Early Latin Hymnaries,*[1] an index of hymns in hymnaries before 1100, has included the hymns which appear in sources from various places in England, France, Germany, Italy and Spain. A few twelfth-century hymnaries have been used also, and a very small number, principally English, which appear later. There are eighty-nine hymns in this index which are found in the Sarum breviary. Thus fresh evidence is afforded of the existence of the traditional hymn cycle and its diffusion. One can tell at a glance the continental setting of eighty-nine of the 119 Sarum hymns and also to what extent several other hymns of the York and Hereford rites were used outside of England.

Mearns' list, however, has not been employed for this purpose primarily, in the present study. It is more valuable as an indication of the hymns which were included in monastic breviaries in England. So far, diocesan liturgies only have been considered, although the monastic tradition has been shown to be very strong in the compilation of their hymnaries. A group of thirty-two important hymns not found in the rites of Sarum, York or Hereford but characteristic of monastic orders, has been chosen from Mearns' list on the basis of their appearance in volumes L and LI of the *Analecta*

Hymnica. As volume L contains the hymns of Blume's supplementary series of leading hymn writers, and volume LI those hymns from Daniel's *Thesaurus* which were written from the fifth to the eleventh centuries, a representative selection of material has been secured as well as easy availability in printed form.

Summing up the discussion of the present chapter, the following points seem clear.

The Latin hymn collections in the breviaries of medieval England were based on a traditional monastic cycle handed down from the sixth century. The primitive cycle was superseded by a ninth-century series in which three principal divisions are apparent, the Proper of the Season, the Common of Saints and the Proper of Saints.

The invention of the sequence in the ninth century resulted in the composition of a large number of new pieces to be employed in connection with the missal. They fall into the same three divisions as do the breviary hymns, i.e. sequences for the Proper of the Season etc.

After the twelfth century, the evolution of hymns and sequences is marked by a greater variety due to the establishment of late medieval feasts and the cults of local saints.

The hymns of the Sarum Use have been selected as the most representative and important of all the medieval hymn collections in England because of the prestige and widespread adoption of the Sarum liturgy. The hymns of the York ritual not occurring in the Sarum Use have been added as representative of the northern part of England and therefore supplementary to the hymns of the Sarum rite which prevailed generally in the south of England. The hymns of the Hereford ritual not occurring in the Sarum or York collections have been chosen as the third group. They are important, partly because of the fame of the diocese and partly because they serve to illustrate more fully the variable element in the collections.   The hymns from Mearns' Index have been chosen as a group characteristic of monastic centers.

The material which has been described above is well adapted to reflect medieval opinion in any sphere of thought related to its subject matter.   It has the advantage of a constant element which had been subjected to a process of selection for many centuries and had reached its established form before the twelfth century.   After the twelfth century it expands along certain lines characteristic of the religious development of the later Middle Ages.

The material selected has an additional advantage for the present study because it represents a very large section of the British Isles.   Finally, it is by no means exclusively English but belongs to the universal medieval church.

The actual number of hymns and sequences used is as follows:

The Sarum collection 231
The York collection 74
The Hereford collection 40
The Winchester Troper 54
       (not in above collections)
The Latin Hymns of the Anglo-Saxon Church 51
       (not in above collections)
Hymns from Mearns' Index 32
       (not in above collections)

                                                                                   —————

Total 482

CHAPTER II

HYMNS FOR THE PROPER OF THE SEASON

I. THE CANONICAL HOURS

THE hymns used in the services of the canonical hours are the very heart of the hymnology of the western church. They pulsate with energy and power derived from the early centuries of struggle, for they were composed and sung by the Christian church of that period. Not only are they important as marking an early stage in the historical development of the hymnal but they also reflect the ethical principles upon which the medieval ideal was founded. Each one of the canonical hours possesses its own symbolism. Each one suggests and reinforces an important moral truth which is part of the ideal Christian life.

Beginning with the vigil of Saturday night in preparation for the following Sunday, the first three centuries of Christian history developed public services for prayer at candle light, night time and dawn. By the fourth century the tide of ascetic influence had set in, bringing with it the daily devotions in the church at the third, sixth and ninth hours. At the end of the fourth and during the fifth century the cycle was completed with new offices at sunrise and nightfall. The full series, therefore, included the nocturnal cursus; vespers, compline, matins (the nocturns and lauds), and the diurnal cursus; prime, terce, sext and nones.[1] An opportunity was afforded to unify the services and at the same time to make use of the symbolic number seven, by reference to Psalm

[1] P. Batiffol, *Histoire du Bréviaire romain*, translated by A. M. Y. Bayley (London: Longmans, Green & Co., 1912), chap. I.

119:164 (Ps. 118, Vulgate) : " Seven times a day do I praise thee because of thy righteous ordinances." A hymn from the primitive cycle expresses the idea thus : " Seven times this day let us sing praises unto the Lord." [1]

From the simple assemblies of early Christianity and the daily offices of prayer observed in monastic and ascetic groups, the fully elaborated liturgy of the hours developed.[2] At first a great variety prevailed in the details of worship but uniformity was secured about the ninth century. By this time day and night offices were observed in cathedral and parish churches as well as in monastic institutions.[3]

The question naturally arises to what extent the laity participated in the services of the canonical hours. If they were to benefit by the moral or religious teachings conveyed, attendance was essential or else the use of books of devotion in private. Evidence bearing upon the problem of Sunday attendance at mass has been presented in another place. On Sundays, matins and vespers at least, were generally attended.[4] During Anglo-Saxon times in England the people are said to have joined in the offices of the hours.[5]

The symbolism of the hour services was a matter of in-

[1] *Postmatutinis laudibus, Anal. Hymn.*, LI, no. 12, lines 13-14.

[2] The words *liturgy* and *liturgical* may be used in two senses. The wider significance refers to a form of worship authorized by the church, to be used in its public services. The special significance refers to the celebration and administration of the Eucharist. The wider meaning is used here and in general throughout this study.

[3] L. Duchesne, *Origines du Culte chrétien*, translated by M. L. McClure, *Christian Worship, its Origin and Evolution* (London: S.P.C.K., 1904), pp. 448-452.

[4] For interesting evidence pointing to attendance by laymen at the services of the Hours, *vide* Gasquet, *Parish Life in Mediaeval England*, chap. vii, *Parish Church Services*; Cutts, *Parish Priests and Their People*, chap. xiii, *Public Services in Church*.

[5] D. Rock, *Church of Our Fathers*, edited by Hart and Frere (London: Hodges, 1903-1904), IV, pp. 16-18.

terest from the beginning. The Scriptures of the Old and New Testaments supplied abundant material to enhance their significance. Ambrose quoted the words of Psalm 119 (118) : 62 as a precedent for prayer in the night. " At midnight I will rise to give thanks unto thee because of thy righteous ordinances." Night and its darkness were conducive to temptation. Paul and Silas, Ambrose reminds the reader, arose and praised God in the night, even in prison (Acts 16:25).[1] So the hymn has it: " We rise to confess thee; we break the night; we lift our thoughts and our hands as we know the prophet did. He commanded us to follow his example and Paul approved it by his acts." [2] Just as midnight is a period of darkness and temptation, so Ambrose thinks of midday as the hour of light and purity of thought.[3] Out of these two concepts which connect the grosser sins with the night and virtue with the day, arose the warning against impurity in the hymns for the nocturnal cursus and the prayer for self-control in the hymns for the diurnal cursus, with which, for this purpose, matins are associated. In general the church encouraged the worshipper, through the medium of morning and evening hymns, to practice restraint and fortitude and to avoid impurity and sloth. Ideals of conduct were further developed as the primitive types of morning and evening worship were transformed into the complete series continuing throughout the twenty-four hours.

During the thirteenth century a well-known canonist and liturgist, Guilelmus Durandus (d. 1296), appeared who wrote a great treatise upon the ceremonies of the church and their symbolic interpretation, *Rationale divinorum officiorum*.[4] Among the reasons Durandus gives for the prayers

---

[1] Ambrose, *Expos. in Ps. 118, Sermo 8* (CSEL, lxii, 8, 45-51).

[2] *Rerum creator optime*, S.B., lines 7-12.

[3] Ambrose, *ibid.* (CSEL, lxii, 51).

[4] Durandus is quoted extensively by Thalhofer from whose work the following account of the canonical hours is taken. *Vide* V. Thalhofer

of the nocturns and lauds are these: that thanks be given for salvation, since the first-born of the Hebrews were saved at night, that the night of human sin may be illuminated and that the sins of the flesh may be exorcised by chanting and prayer.   Not only do the hymns reflect this attitude but they contain words which indicate their use during the usual sleeping hours.   " It is the dead of night.   The prophet's voice enjoins us ever to give praises to God the Father and the Son."   " This is the hour of safety for the justified and for those whom the death angel dared not strike, fearing the sign of blood." [1]

The first emphasis noticeable in the hymns for matins, is placed upon the avoidance of sloth.   Sloth is not only laziness or indolence or inactivity.   It manifests itself in sluggishness and in indifference to things spiritual, in neglect of duty and love of ease.   It is felt also in the discontent or weariness which was apt to result from the monastic routine. " Banishing sloth afar let us all arise quickly." [2]   " With strength refreshed by sleep, spurning the couch, we rise." [3] " Free us, who have been sunk in sleep, from harmful love of repose." [4]   " Banish drowsiness lest it overwhelm us in indolence." [5]   Such are the characteristic expressions of the repudiation of sloth.   One might regard them as the inevitable convention of morning hymns, did not sloth appear as a definite sin in other connotations.   " Behold the slug-

and Eisenhofer, *Handbuch der katholischen Liturgik* (Freiburg im Breisgau: Herder, 1912), II, pp. 574-615; Durandus, *Rationale divinorum officiorum* (Lugduni, 1612), I, l. 5, cc. 3-10.

[1] *Mediae noctis tempus est, Anal. Hymn.*, LI, no. 1, stanzas 1, 4.   Other citations showing the use of the hymns at night are as follows: *Nocte surgentes vigilemus omnes*, S.B., line 1; *Consors paterni luminis*, S.B., line 3; *Tu trinitatis unitas*, S.B., lines 5, 6.

[2] *Primo dierum omnium*, S.B., lines 5, 6.

[3] *Somno refectis artubus*, S.B., lines 1, 2.

[4] *Rerum creator optime*, S.B., lines 3, 4.

[5] *Consors paterni luminis*, S.B., lines 7, 8.

gishness of the sinful mind which poisonous guilt is sting-
ing." [1] " Let not our hearts be indifferent nor any stain of
sin cool the ardor of the soul." [2] " May our God taking pity
upon us, banish our languor and grant us spiritual health." [3]

All the emphasis is not placed, however, upon the negative
aspect of the ideal life. Watchfulness, forceful activity and
courage are unmistakably enjoined as an offset to sloth. The
loins must be girded in the Old Testament spiritual sense [4]
and the soul must be continually on guard. [5] The heavenly
father grants the strength for strenuous action. [6] Ambrose
had struck this militant note in the earliest period of Latin
hymnology and Prudentius, too, had written of the challenge
to activity suggested by the dawn of a new day. Both employed at length the symbolism of the crowing cock herald-
ing the day, in two of the best-known Latin hymns, *Aeterne
rerum conditor* (Ambrose) and *Ales diei nuntius* (Prudentius). To the mind of Prudentius the cock crow symbolized
the call of Jesus to the soul, a summons not only to watchfulness and activity but to purity, righteousness and sobriety of
life. Ambrose amplifies the theme, reminding the worshipper of that night throng of evil spirits which the crowing
cock was powerful to dispel. To the people of the Middle
Ages, as to those of pagan antiquity and to many of our
contemporaries, the demon world was an ever present reality.
It was a part of their mental background. The particular
superstition associated with the cock crow was destined to
survive for centuries. [7] Other morning hymns besides the
two just mentioned contain variations of the same metaphor.

[1] *Nox atra rerum contegit*, S.B., lines 9, 10.
[2] *Tu trinitatis unitas*, S.B., lines 14-16.
[3] *Ecce iam noctis tenuatur umbra, S.B.*, lines 5, 6.
[4] *Summae deus clementiae*, S.B., line 11.
[5] *Ales diei nuntius*, S.B., line 8.
[6] *Splendor paternae gloriae*, S.B., line 13.
[7] For the significance of the cock crow in a later period *vide* Shake-
speare, *Hamlet*, Act I, Scene I, lines 148-156.

Not only do morning hymns require the worshipper to shun indolence and to cultivate earnestness but they point the way to purity of thought, word and action.   " Grant that the father may govern and control the mind of him whose acts are pure and loyal." [1]   " We know thee, alone, O Christ, when the mind is pure and guileless." [2]   " That with hearts free from stain, we may enjoy thee more fully." [3]   " Stretch out thy right hand to us as we rise, and let the mind be sober and eager for the praise of God." [4]

Departure from the ideal of purity is condemned.   Both the virtue and the contrasting sin are reflected in the following: " May this day preserve us pure.—Let not the shifting eye look upon sin nor the body be stained with evil." [5]   The vigilance of him whose loins are girded is a continual defense against the evil of excess.[6]   Other illustrations of this idea abound.   " Grant that the flesh be not unclean." [7] " May unclean desire be far from us and every evil act." [8]

So far, sloth and impurity of every sort have been condemned in morning hymns, while courageous action and purity in all their forms have been approved.   Other qualities of the heart and life are also praised or blamed as the case may be.   " Let us say nothing deceitful, let us ponder no dark thought.". . .   " Let not the tongue nor hand be false." This is a single reference, however, to deceit, whereas other forms of disapproved conduct have been repeatedly men-

[1] *Splendor paternae gloriae*, S.B., lines 17-18.

[2] *Nox et tenebrae et nubila*, S.B., lines 9, 10.

[3] *Summae deus clementiae*, S.B., lines 7, 8.

[4] *Aeterna caeli gloria*, S.B., lines 5-8.

[5] *Lux ecce surgit aurea*, S.B., lines 5-6, 11-12.

[6] *Summae deus clementiae*, S.B., lines 11-12.

[7] *Tu trinitatis unitas*, S.B., line 13.

[8] *Primo dierum omnium*, S.B., lines 19-20.

[9] *Lux ecce surgit aurea*, S.B., lines 7, 8, 10.

tioned. The virtues other than courage or purity which are most frequently praised, are those of faith, hope and love, sometimes separately and sometimes as a trilogy. Once more the cock crow is the signal for returning hope and faith.[1] One hymn has three different petitions for faith. " May faith be warm and glowing.—May Christ be our food and faith be our drink.—May faith be like the noonday." [2] Faith, hope and love are combined as follows: " Now first may faith, already sought, be rooted deeply within our beings. Then may hope rejoice with faith that greater love may arise." [3]

Matins, including the nocturns and lauds, is followed by prime, a formal service of morning prayer which constitutes a dedication for the day. It is the appropriate hour to shake off sloth and to resolve upon self-control, moderation and purity of heart. These are lessons already familiar from illustrations cited above, but in the hymn for prime, *Iam lucis orto sidere,* a new theme appears. Not only purity of heart but other forms of moderation and self-control are the objects of petition. " May he, bridling the tongue, restrain our speech lest the horror of strife resound. May he cover the eyes with cherishing love lest they behold vanities. May our hearts be pure within and all madness flee away. Let moderation in food and drink wear away the pride of the flesh; that when the day has gone and fate brings back the night, pure by reason of abstinence we may sing his glory." [4] It will be observed that two sins, namely, strife and pride are mentioned for the first time, while the virtue of self-control has been greatly enriched in significance, by emphasis upon new aspects.

[1] *Aeterne rerum conditor,* S.B., lines 21, 24.

[2] *Splendor paternae gloriae,* S.B., lines 19, 21-22, 27.

[3] *Aeterna caeli gloria,* S.B., lines 21-24.

[4] *Iam lucis orto sidere,* S.B., lines 4-12.

Terce, the third hour, marks the descent of the Holy Spirit
(Acts 2:15). Its hymns are full of Pentecostal fervor and
of that love for God and man which is the Spirit's peculiar
gift. The third hour brings to mind, also, the condemnation of Jesus and salvation from sin. " At this third hour,
O Christ, fill us with thy grace and make us and those nearest
fervent with love. May God the Paraclete now be present
in our hearts, in this hour which inflamed the apostles glowing with tongues of fire." [1] A hymn addressed to the Holy
Spirit reflects the love which, once received, finds its own
object of devotion. " Let word, tongue, mind, heart, strength
sound forth their confession. Let love flame up with fire
and the soul's warmth kindle its neighbor." [2] Suggestive of
the familiar words of Deuteronomy 6:5, " Thou shalt love
the Lord thy God with all thine heart and with all thy soul,
and with all thy might ", it contains also the wider application of that same thought found in Matthew 20:37, 39:
" Thou shalt love the Lord thy God with all thy heart, and
with all thy soul, and with all thy mind ", and again: " Thou
shalt love thy neighbor as thyself." It will be remembered
that *proximus* is the word for " neighbor " in the Vulgate.
Walpole is of the opinion that *igne* in this stanza definitely recalls the Pentecostal flame.[3] Granting these assumptions,
one stanza of four lines contains within itself the fully
rounded ideal of love as a virtue, its origin and its appropriate
expression. Faith and hope are combined with love as follows: " By the faith of God in which we live, by the everlast-

[1] *Christe hac hora tertia*, D.H., stanzas 1, 2. The following reflects
the condemnation of Jesus: *Dei fide qua vivimus*, D.H., stanza 2.

[2]   Os, lingua, mens, sensus, vigor,
    Confessionem personent
    Flammescat igne caritas,
    Accendat ardor proximos.
        Nunc sancte nobis spiritus, S.B., stanza 2.

[3] A. S. Walpole, *Early Latin Hymns*, pp. 108-110.

ing hope in which we believe, by the grace of love, let us sing praises to Christ." [1]

Hymns for terce contain the nucleus of the theme of love as a Christian virtue, which was to be greatly elaborated in all hymns associated with the feast of Pentecost. Further consideration of the subject, therefore, must be postponed for the Proper of the Season.

The sixth hour, sext, is high noon. The sun is at its zenith. It suggests the heat of evil and the flames of strife. " Powerful ruler and God of truth, who dost control the changes of day and night, thou dost furnish the day with splendor and noon with fire. Extinguish the flames of strife, banish the heat of evil, grant us health of body and true peace of heart." [2] This is the hour which commemorates the sufferings of the crucifixion,—a thought which finds expression in a mid-day hymn, giving added emphasis to the usual symbolism of the hour. " May Christ enrich with a thirst for righteousness those who sing his praises at the hour when he thirsted and suffered on the cross. May pride be sinful and virtue a desire to those who feel a hunger which he alone satisfies. Thus may the gift of the Holy Spirit be poured upon those who sing praises, that the heat of the flesh may be cooled and the coolness of the spirit glow with new warmth." [3] Let it be noted here that pride is considered a sin sufficiently abhorrent to be contrasted with virtue itself, and that impurity and indifference are the two sins marked for cleansing by the Holy Spirit.

The lengthening shadows of the afternoon mark the ninth hour or nones. It is the time when Peter and John entered the temple to pray. It brings the connotation of sorrow for wrong done during the day, of continued effort toward sin-

[1] *Dei fide qua vivimus*, D.H., stanza 1.
[2] *Rector potens verax deus*, S.B., stanzas 1, 2.
[3] *Qua Christus hora sitiit*, D.H., stanzas 1-3.

lessness, and of the afternoon of life. " At the season of the ninth hour, the perfect three times three, singing due praises we chant our hymns; holding fast the sacred mystery of God with pure hearts, the example taught us by Peter, handed down for a sign of safety." [1] " Grant us an unclouded evening that life may not fail in strength, but may eternal glory follow, the reward of a holy death." [2]

Vespers at sunset, and compline at nightfall, complete the series of canonical hours. Incidentally, the symbolic value of the number seven was further enhanced in the vesper liturgy by a group of hymns commemorating the six days of creation and the seventh of rest. The greater number of vesper hymns, however, reflect the passing day and approaching night, contrition for sin and desire for protection and purity during the hours of darkness. " Now the close of the last hour of day ushers in the evening. The sun proclaims by its setting that night is at hand." [3] In the final hymns for the day the desire for purity seems uppermost. Prudentius would have the Christian banish the temptations of the night by the mystic power which lies in the sign of the cross.[4] The unknown author of *Salvator mundi domine* has expressed the thought of the evening hymn in a more conventional manner, and with great simplicity. " Let sleep overcome folly, let not the enemy surprise us, nor let the flesh, we beseech thee, be stained by any impurity. With the sacrifices of the heart, we pray thee, who dost transform the senses, that with pure minds we may arise from sleep." [5] Another evening hymn gathers up into one stanza the twofold character of impurity, the desire within and its expression

[1] *Perfecto trino numero, D.H.,* stanzas 1, 2.

[2] *Rerum deus tenax vigor, S.B.,* stanza 2.

[3] *Iam ter quarternis trahitur, Y.B.,* stanza 1.

[4] *Cultor dei, memento, S.B.,* stanza 2.

[5] *Salvator mundi domine, S.B.,* stanzas 3, 4.

in outward acts. " Repel from thy servants whatever, due to impurity, suggests itself in their conduct or enters into their actions." [1] Again, " Let not heavy sleep nor the enemy surprise us. Let not the flesh in agreement with him, cause us to be culprits in thy sight." [2]

As at mid-day, there is a warning at evening against strife.[3] Boasting too, is condemned.[4] On the side of the virtues, obedience and faith are praised.[5] Obedience, which one might expect to be much emphasized, receives surprisingly little attention in the hymns anywhere, while faith must be regarded as a supreme virtue if frequency of mention is to be trusted as an indication of its importance. The prominence of faith will be considered later.

In summing up the teachings conveyed by the hymns used in connection with the canonical hours, two compositions of Ambrose will be quoted in full; the first, *Aeterne rerum conditor* for the morning and the second, *Deus creator omnium* for the evening.

> Aeterne rerum conditor,
> Noctem diemque qui regis,
> Et temporum das tempora,
> Ut alleves fastidium.

> Praeco diei iam sonet,
> Noctis profundae pervigil,
> Nocturna lux viantibus,
> A nocte noctem segregans.

[1] *Plasmator hominis deus*, S.B., stanza 3.

[2] *Christe qui lux es et dies*, S.B., stanza 3.

[3] *Plasmator hominis deus*, S.B., lines 15, 16.

[4] *Magnus deus potentiae*, S.B., line 14.

[5] *Telluris ingens conditor*, S.B., line 13. *Immense caeli conditor*, S.B., stanza 4.

Hoc excitatus lucifer,
Solvit polum caligine,
Hoc omnis errorum chorus
Viam nocendi deserit.

Hoc nauta vires colligit,
Pontique mitescunt freta :
Hoc ipsa petra ecclesiae
Canente culpam diluit.

Surgamus ergo strenue,
Gallus iacentes excitat,
Et somnolentos increpat,
Gallus negantes arguit.

Gallo canente spes redit,
Aegris salus refunditur,
Mucro latronis conditur,
Lapsis fides revertitur.

Jesu labentes respice,
Et nos videndo corrige ;
Si respicis lapsi stabunt,
Fletuque culpa solvitur.

Tu lux refulge sensibus,
Mentisque somnum discute,
Te nostra vox primum sonet,
Et vota solvamus tibi.[1]

[1] " 1. Eternal founder of the universe who dost rule the night and day and dost bestow the changes of the seasons to relieve weariness ; 2. Now let the herald of the day sound forth, vigilant throughout the depth of night, a light in the darkness to wayfarers, separating the watches of the night. 3. At his voice the sun, awakened, clears the sky of clouds. At his voice the whole throng of evil spirits desert the path of harm. 4. At his voice the sailor gathers strength, and the waves of the sea are calmed. At his voice, the Rock of the church himself washes away his sin. 5. Therefore, let us arise in vigor. The cock arouses the indolent, rebukes the sleepy, and denounces those who deny. 6. At the cock crow hope returns, health is restored to the sick, the dagger of the thief is sheathed

Deus creator omnium,
Polique rector vestiens
Diem decoro lumine,
Noctem soporis gratia.

Artus solutos ut quies,
Reddat laboris usui,
Mentesque fessas allevet,
Luctusque solvat anxios.

Grates peracto iam die,
Et noctis exortu preces,
Votis reos ut adiuves,
Hymnum canentes solvimus.

Te cordis ima concinant,
Te vox canora concrepet,
Te diligat castus amor,
Te mens adoret sobria.

Ut cum profundo clauserit,
Diem caligo noctium,
Fides tenebras nesciat,
Et nox fidei luceat.

Dormire mentem ne sinas,
Dormire culpa noverit,
Castos fides refrigerans,
Somni vaporem temperet.

Exuta sensu lubrico,
Te cordis alta somnient,
Ne hostis invidi dolo,
Pavor quietos suscitet.[1]

and faith comes back to the fallen. 7. Jesus, do thou regard us, wavering, and by thy look amend our ways. If thou dost look upon us, the fallen will rise up again and sin be effaced with tears. 8. Shine, thou light, upon our senses, disperse the sleep of the mind. Let our voices resound first to thy praise and let us pay our vows to thee."

[1] "1. O God, creator of all things, and ruler of the heavens, clothing the day with brightness and the night with the grace of sleep. 2. That rest

St. Augustine mentions the above hymns as the work of Ambrose [1] while other hymns of the hour series have been assigned to the same author on various grounds, with a high degree of probability. They are *Splendor paternae gloriae, Nunc sancte nobis spiritus, Rector potens verax deus,* and *Rerum deus tenax vigor.*[2] The authenticity of hymns doubtfully attributed to Ambrose is, after all, a matter of little consequence. The point is that a large number of medieval Latin hymns reflect the spirit and ideals which are discovered in the compositions definitely known to be his. He had a host of imitators. Whatever the influence of Ambrose may have been upon medieval theology, through his prose writings, his hymns, both as to metrical form and subject matter, set the standard for centuries. He does not, chronologically speaking, belong to the Middle Ages for he lived in the borderland which lies between them and the Roman imperial period. He was an exponent of the cardinal virtues of the pagan past and he helped to impress them upon the medieval future. "Nor do we fail presently to observe how truly these poems belonged to their time and the circumstances under which they were produced—how suitably the faith which was in actual conflict with, and was just triumphing

may restore wearied limbs for their accustomed toil, relieve exhausted minds, and relax torturing cares. 3. Now at the close of day and the approach of night, we pour out in hymns our thanks and our prayers, that thou shouldst aid us who made our vows to thee. 4. Let the depth of the heart praise thee, let the tuneful voice sound thy praise, let pure love cherish thee and the sober mind adore thee. 5. That when the mists of night cover the day in their depths, faith may know no darkness, but may the night be illumined with faith. 6. Let not the soul sleep, for sin may bring its taint to the sleeper. Let faith refreshing the chaste, cool the warm breath of sleep. 7. With deceitful sense put off, let the depths of the heart dream of thee, lest by the trickery of the envious foe, trembling seize upon those at rest."

[1] A. S. Walpole, *Early Latin Hymns*, p. 23.

[2] A. S. Walpole, *ibid.*, pp. 35, 108.

over, the powers of this world, found its utterance in hymns
such as these, wherein is no softness, perhaps little tender-
ness : but in place of these a rock-like firmness, the old Roman
stoicism transmuted and glorified into that nobler Christian
courage, which encountered and at length overcame the
world." [1]

In the sense that Ambrose helped to form the thought of
medieval Christianity, he may be said to be medieval. In
the morning and evening hymns he accepts with enthusiasm
the four great Pagan and the three Christian virtues, revealing his hatred for the sins which are their opposites. " Ambrose has an ethical program which sweeps over Pagan principles and Christian deeds." [2] Other evidences of his influence will be apparent later. In a similar way, Prudentius
(b. 348) placed his impress upon medieval Latin hymnology.
In the hour group there are *Ales diei nuntius, Nox et tenebrae et nubila, Lux ecce surgit aurea* and *Cultor dei memento,*
all of them centos taken from his *Cathemerinon* or daily
hymn-book intended for private use.[3] The influence of Prudentius was extraordinary in the Middle Ages, not only in
hymnology but through his well-known allegorical poems
Psychomachia and *Hamartigenia,* which describe the struggle
of virtues and sins for supremacy over the soul of man.[4]

The hymns for the canonical hours representing the earliest
period of Latin hymnology, have yielded definite information as to the leading virtues which helped to make up the
Christian ideal and the sins which were alien to it. They

---

[1] R. C. Trench, *Sacred Latin Poetry* (London: Macmillan, 1874), p. 88.

[2] E. K. Rand, *Founders of the Middle Ages* (Cambridge: Harvard
Univ. Press, 1928), p. 82.

[3] A. S. Walpole, *op. cit.,* p. 115 *et seq.* E. K. Rand, *op. cit.,* pp. 207-213.

[4] In the *Psychomachia* (verses 21 *et seq.*) he lines up the antagonists as
follows: *Fides* vs. *Veterum Cultura Deorum, Pudicitia* vs. *Libido,
Patientia* vs. *Ira, Humilitas* vs. *Superbia, Sobrietas* vs. *Luxuria, Operatio*
vs. *Avaritia, Concordia* vs. *Discordia.*

are, on the one hand, self-control and purity in various forms, courageous activity and vigilance, faith, hope and love; on the other hand, they are impurity and excess, indifference and sloth, pride and boasting, and strife. It will be interesting to compare this ideal which appears to be evolving in liturgical hymns, with two remarkable poems of the same period, *Rex deus immense,* a hymn by Eugenius of Toledo (d. 658) and Bede's great hymn on the six days of creation, *Primo deus coeli globum,* which closes with a prayer. The opening lines of the former constitute a fervent plea to be granted the chief virtues. " O mighty God and king, by whom the universe is established, mercifully grant the prayer of Eugenius, thy wretched servant. May true faith be mine without false doctrines, and especially may my conduct be amended. Make me loving, humble, true, prudent, silent and careful of speech. Make me a faithful comrade and ever a loyal friend. Grant that I may be a minister of thine, kind, sober, temperate and pure." The second part of the hymn is a repudiation of the chief sins.   " May riches be far from me, pride and wranglings of strife, envy, excess and gluttony, lest I injure any man through sin or be myself its victim." [1] Bede prays thus for virtue: " Let our hearts be pure and brave, let the flesh be very sparing, let the spirit glow like the sun and never be lukewarm. Let love, twofold, conferring the twin wings of the virtues, render its own image like that of its creator." [2]

The hymns of Eugenius and of Bede are in virtual agreement with the hour hymns upon matters of sin and of the ideal life. Eugenius, in particular, has listed in one poem several virtues and sins which receive frequent emphasis in the canonical group, although not in one place. The list of sins which he indicates is of special interest, comprising avar-

[1] *Rex deus immense, Anal. Hymn.,* 50, no. 73, lines 1-8, 11-13.
[2] *Primo deus coeli globum, Anal. Hymn.,* L, no. 80, stanzas 30, 31.

ice, pride, strife, envy, impurity and gluttony. Bede, on the other hand, lists the virtues only, placing together those which have chiefly characterized the hour hymns. It seems clear that the authors of all these hymns had in mind certain specific qualities with which they were familiar and were in turn impressing upon others through the medium of religious verse. They taught the existence of certain ideals by which to measure good and evil conduct, but they did not create the standard which they presented in their poetry. The hymns reflect a point of view which was current in contemporary theological opinion and thus they establish the claim made by Father Blume that hymnology is a guide to the ideas and ideals of medieval life.

The term "standard" is capable of various interpretations, but for the present purpose it may be defined in the words of J. H. Muirhead in an article on *Ethics* in the *Encyclopedia of Religion and Ethics*. He thus indicates the scope of his subject: "Its subject matter is human conduct and character, not as actual facts with a history and causal connexions with other facts, but as possessing value in view of a standard or ideal." What is the "standard or ideal" in view of which human conduct and character possessed value, in the minds of the hymn writers? What combination of virtues made the ideal? What qualities were to be avoided by those who would strive for perfection? In order to answer this question, it becomes necessary to leave the hymnal entirely and to follow the course of early medieval opinion upon the subject of what constitutes the chief virtues and the chief sins. As this inquiry proceeds, it will appear that from the early Christian centuries lists of virtues and sins were extant, at first variable, but gradually merged into the definite form of seven principal virtues and seven deadly sins. There can be no reasonable doubt that men who knew what the leaders of the church were teaching about this subject, would express in their hymns ideas consistent with the thought of the age. But hymns should be lyric, not didactic, in their nature. A freer treatment is characteristic of them. Formal lists such as those of Bede and Eugenius are rare. Still, a striking correspondence will be observed between the ideal qualities mentioned in the early hymns and the conventional teachings set forth in expository works of the same period.

The notion of seven principal virtues and seven deadly sins is in part a heritage from classical antiquity and in part a survival of early Christian beliefs. Only the first stages of its evolution will be traced at this point, as it will be necessary to review the greater number of hymns antedating 1100, before presenting the standard in its completed form as generally accepted in the twelfth century.

Socrates was influential in making effective the idea of four leading virtues, namely, *wisdom, courage, temperance* and *justice*. Aristotle treated them as the mean between two extremes, but the Stoics returned to the thought of the four positive values.[1] The theory of four passions and four evils, counterparts of the four virtues, is said to have been taught by Zeno: *sorrow, fear, inordinate desire* and *sensuous pleasure* being passions, and *folly, cowardice, intemperance* and *injustice* being evils, a system of eight concepts in all. The whole forms the basis of the pagan ethical system as completed before the rise of Christianity.[2] Philo of Alexandria first attempted to support the theory of four virtues by proof from the Bible, likening them to the four streams of paradise.[3] It was Ambrose, however, who as-

[1] O. Zöckler, *Die Tugendlehre des Christentums* (Gütersloh: Bertelsmann, 1904), pp. 22, 26 *et seq.*, 32 *et seq.*

[2] O. Zöckler, *Das Lehrstück von den sieben Hauptsünden* (München: Beck, 1893), pp. 5, 6.

[3] Philo, *Allegoriae Legum*, i, 19; edited by L. Cohn, *Philonis Opera* (Berlin: Reimer, 1896), I, 77.

similated them to Christian thought and who was the first to apply the term *cardinal* to the four pagan virtues.[1] He discusses the subject in his *De officiis* and *De paradiso,* in the second of which he reconciles the pagan virtues to Christianity by tracing them to their source Jesus Christ, *fons vitae aeternae,* once more under the symbol of the four streams of paradise.[2]

Another influence which contributed to the evolution of the ideal was that of Neoplatonism which developed the idea of stages of virtue, powerfully reinforcing Christianity by asserting the relation of the practice of virtue to the knowledge of God.[3] The ancient system, however, as derived from the philosophers of Greece lacked the consciousness of sin which was imparted by the Christian belief in a divinely revealed plan of salvation.[4] Meantime, Christianity had emphasized the three virtues of *faith, hope* and *love,* but the addition of these to the four pagan virtues as a group of seven did not take place until much later. Clement of Alexandria (b. 150?), for instance, discusses both groups but not as a unified system.[5] Augustine, also, discusses the virtues. He mentions them all but never lists them together, for his interest is centered upon the ultimate principle upon which they rest rather than upon the groups as such. To him the love of God is the common source from which all the virtues spring and the principle by which they are united.[6]

[1] Ambrose, *In Lucam,* v, 62 (PL, xv, 1653).

[2] Ambrose, *De paradiso,* 3 (PL, xiv, 279-280 or CSEL, xxxii, 1, pp. 272-274) ; *De officiis,* i, 24, 115 (PL, xvi, 57).

[3] O. Zöckler, *Die Tugendlehre des Christentums,* p. 41.

[4] O. Zöckler, *ibid.,* p. 43.

[5] O. Zöckler, *ibid.,* p. 47.

[6] Augustine, *De moribus ecclesiae,* i, 15 (PL, xxxii, 1322) ; *Enarratio in psalmum 83:8* (PL, xxxvii, 1065-1066) ; *De civitate Dei,* iv, 21 (PL, xli, 127-129 or CSEL, xl, 1, 188-190) ; *De civitate Dei,* xii, 6 (PL, xli, 553 or CSEL, xl, 1, 573) ; *De civitate Dei,* xix, 25 (PL, xli, 656 or CSEL, xl, 2, 420).

As symbolism was to exert so great an influence upon
teaching regarding the virtues, it seems strange that the interest of the number seven did not immediately assert itself
in a combination of the four cardinal virtues and the three
theological virtues, as faith, hope and love came to be termed.
That was reserved for a later period and was the result of
the symbolism of the seven gifts of the Holy Spirit, as will
appear in another connection.   The symbolic treatment of
the cardinal virtues was continued by Julianus Pomerius (c.
480).   Adopting the idea of the four rivers of paradise, he
also uses the comparison of four elements, four points of the
compass, four evangelists and so forth.[1]   So the cardinal and
theological groups lived on side by side, firmly rooted in
Christian thought and without variation in the specific units
of which they were composed, i.e., the group comprising courage, justice, moderation and prudence, and the group comprising faith, hope and love.

Very different was the case with the lists of sins which had
their starting point in the four passions and four evils of
Zeno.   These had been discussed and elaborated by Roman
authors.   Cicero presents the four passions of Zeno as *aegri-
tudo, metus, libido* and *voluptas,* showing the evil qualities
which spring from them.[2]   They are implied in the writings
of Virgil.[3]   Roman literature, too, had made an additional
contribution to the subject when Horace described the characteristics which had no place in the life of virtue or wisdom,
namely, avarice, cupidity, pride, envy, wrath, inactivity, excess in drinking, and lust.

Not only in pagan but in Christian writings the specific
qualities varied from list to list, and the total number of
seven was finally fixed upon only after a long rivalry with

---

[1] Julianus Pomerius, *De vita contemplativa,* iii, 18 (PL, lix, 501).

[2] Cicero, *Tusc. Quaest.* IV, 6 *et seq.*

[3] *Hinc metuunt cupiuntque, dolent gaudentque,*... (Aen. VI, 732).

[4] Horace, *Epis.* I, 1, 33-40.

eight. Moreover the ten commandments of the Hebrew Scriptures provided the Christian with a complete ethical standard which was influential in forming lists of sins. Tertullian (b. 160?), for instance, shows his dependence upon the Old Testament source in a comparison of the nation of Israel to Naaman the Leper, in which he mentions seven chief sins, namely, idolatry, blasphemy, murder, adultery, defilement, false witness and fraud.[1] Origen (b. 185) in his twelfth homily on the Book of Joshua offers a comparison which was to become more popular than Tertullian's, that is, the seven nations opposing the Israelites in the conquest of Canaan, as types of sin attacking the soul.[2] His list, which he mentions in the first homily, consists of wrath, pride, envy, lust, avarice, iniquity, and like sins (*ceteraque similia*), related partly to pagan and partly to Christian sources.[3] Lust was condemned in both. Pride and avarice were regarded with abhorrence by the idealists of the ancient world, while covetousness was expressly forbidden in the tenth commandment.

Monachism determined which of the two sources should provide the final standard, offering as it did a channel for the spread of ethical ideals. Evagrius Ponticus (d. 398), a hermit of the Egyptian desert, discusses eight states of the soul out of which sins arise. They are gluttony, impurity, avarice, melancholy, wrath, sloth, vain glory and pride. His list is suggested chiefly by the needs of monastic life.[4] Nilus of Constantinople (d. 430) also uses the scheme of eight sins, namely, gluttony, impurity, avarice, wrath, melancholy, sloth, vain glory and pride.[5] The only difference between the lists appears in the Latin where Evagrius employs

[1] Tertullian, *Adv. Marc.*, iv, 9 (PL, ii, 375 or CSEL, xlvii, 441).
[2] Origen, *Homiliae in librum Jesu Nave*, xii (PG, xii, 887).
[3] Origen, *ibid.*, i (PG, xii, 833).
[4] O. Zöckler, *Das Lehrstück von den sieben Hauptsünden*, p. 16 *et seq.*
[5] Nilus, *De octo spiritibus malitiae* (PG, lxxix, 1145-1164).

the words *gula* and *vana gloria* respectively, for gluttony and
vain glory, whereas Nilus speaks of *gastrimargia* and
cenodoxia. In this same period Augustine discusses sins, assigning their common origin to pride, but he does not list
them. His contribution to the subject is a principle of uni-
fication, just as in the case of the virtues he finds their source
in the love of God.

Cassian of Marseilles (d. 435?), whose efforts for the pro-
motion of monastic life and ideals constituted one of the most
important developments in the early history of the institu-
tion, continued the tradition of Evagrius and Nilus. Serapion, however, a priest and abbot living in the Egyptian
desert, was Cassian's immediate inspiration. There are
several persons of the name of Serapion more or less prominent in early Christianity. The hermit whom Cassian
quotes, was a solitary of Scete interviewed by him as he
traveled about Egypt visiting the famous anchorites of the
desert.[1] Serapion's views are set forth in the *Collationes* of
Cassian. Cassian mentions eight principal sins, gluttony,
fornication, vain glory, pride, avarice, wrath, melancholy and
sloth. These he ingeniously harmonizes with the seven requisite for the comparison with the seven enemies of Israel
in Canaan by likening gluttony to Egypt. The land where
Israel had sojourned in captivity had first to be abandoned
before Canaan was entered and conquered. So gluttony, an
elementary condition of the soul, is the first evil to be overcome. Essentially monastic in his outlook, it is not surprising that Cassian devoted a large portion of his *De institutis
coenobiorum* to the consideration of the principal sins, in-
evitably those to the commission of which monachism was
most tempted.[2]

[1] *Vide* Wace and Piercy, *Dictionary of Christian Biography to the End
of the Sixth Century* (London: Murray, 1911).

[2] Cassian, *Collationes,* V, *Conlatio Abbatis Sarapionis: De octo vitiis
principalibus* (CSEL, xiii, 119-151). Also, *De instutitis coenobiorum,* v-
xii (CSEL, xvii, 78-231).

Such was the state of opinion regarding the groups of virtues and sins as it had been formulated prior to the pontificate of Gregory the Great. His occupancy of the papal chair forms a convenient boundary line to mark off the first period in the development of the lists of seven virtues and seven sins. The two groups of cardinal and theological virtues were determined, but not welded together. The lists of sins varied as to both number and selection but the monastic ideal had impressed itself upon them and they awaited some master hand to mould them into final shape. The reflection of thought and discussion which must have accompanied the formation of such lists of virtues and sins is being clearly revealed in the hymns. But they, too, are so far indeterminate. The hymns for the canonical hours are uneven in their emphasis upon the virtues and sins which had been listed and, in some cases, notably prudence and avarice, there is no mention of the qualities concerned. They convey, however, a very definite teaching which is an integral part of the ideal as a whole, just as the hymns are an integral part of a liturgical system which must be surveyed in its entirety before its full meaning is disclosed.

The contribution made to the Christian ideal by the teachings of the hymns for the canonical hours will be more clearly understood after all the hymns in the Proper of the Season have yielded their respective quotas to the ethical standard which is under discussion. At the close of the following chapter, which concludes the treatment of this large group of hymns, a more extended summary of all its parts will be offered.

CHAPTER III

II. SPECIAL FEAST DAYS

ADVENT includes the lesson of the coming judgment. The soul must be purified and ready for the appearance of the divine judge. In this way the season is related to ideals of conduct. Three great Advent hymns from the Sarum breviary bear this teaching, *Conditor alme siderum, Verbum supernum prodiens* and *Vox clara ecce intonat,* perhaps best expressed in the second which suggests the judgment scene as portrayed in Matthew 25:31-46. " And thou shalt afterwards come as judge to open up the secrets of the breast, requiting the evil in accordance with their iniquities and restoring the kingdom to the just in accordance with their good deeds." [1] The same idea is prominent in sequences for Advent.[2] Naturally, therefore, Advent is a challenge to the cultivation of virtue. " Now let the stricken mind arise which lies wounded by evil." [3] " Illumine now our hearts and kindle them with love of thee. When the summons sounds, let deceitful sins be forever banished." [4]

No one virtue is emphasized in hymns like the above, but with the Nativity the case is different. Faith and hope are justified and strengthened by the Incarnation.[5] Purity of heart and conscience are necessary accompaniments for the

[1] *Verbum supernum prodiens,* S.B., stanza 3.

[2] *Salus aeterna,* S.M., line 14. *Regnantem sempiterna,* S.M., line 4.

[3] *Vox clara ecce intonat,* S.B., lines 5, 6.

[4] *Verbum supernum prodiens,* S.B., stanza 2.

[5] *Veni redemptor gentium,* S.B., line 28. *Laude canora vox pulchra,* W.T., lines 6, 13.

worship of the new-born Child,[1] and are strongly suggested
by the Virgin mother, "the royal court of modesty", as
Ambrose calls her.[2] But the greatest of all the virtues suggested by Nativity hymns is that of humility, taught by the
divine example. "He was willing", says Sedulius, "to lie
in the hay; He did not shrink from the manger."[3] The
Sarum missal offers a variant of the same idea. "The
king of the heavens is found among the kine; the king who
encircles all creation lies in a narrow manger."[4] A more
extended form of this theme is found in a hymn by Fortunatus in the York breviary, which opens with the line *Adam
vetus quod polluit*. It will be quoted at length because even
at this early period, the praise of humility is presented as the
offset to pride, a lesson frequently taught in later hymns.
"What the old Adam defiled the new Adam has cleansed.
What the first cast down in pride the second has raised up in
great humility. He who is the author of light was willing to
be placed in a manger. He, who with his Father established
the heavens, wears swaddling clothes under a mother's
care."[5] Humility, so stressed by the hymns of the Nativity
season, is felt to be a requisite for the worshipper. "Let
us most humbly give due praises to the Son, beseeching his
mercy."[6] The humble surroundings of the birth of Jesus
are closely associated with the ideal of poverty which made
so deep an impression upon medieval life. There is but a
hint, so far, of the important place which this aspect of the
ascetic ideal was to hold in the minds of medieval Christians
and, by reflection, in their hymns.

[1] *Gloriosa dies adest*, W.T., lines 7, 8.
[2] Pudoris aula regia, *Veni redemptor gentium*, S.B., line 14.
[3] *A solis ortus cardine*, S.B., lines 21, 22.
[4] *Caeleste organum hodie sonuit*, S.M., lines 15, 16.
[5] *Adam vetus quod polluit*, Y.B., stanzas 1, 5 (Walpole, p. 197).
[6] *Christi hodierna celebremus*, S.M., line 13.

Within the octave of Christmas was celebrated the feast of the Holy Innocents, commemorating the sufferings of the children put to death by Herod in his desire to slay the Christ Child.   They are with good reason considered the first martyrs of the church and Herod, the first persecutor.   In one of the earliest hymns of the church, often attributed to Hilary of Poitiers, occurs the nucleus of the story.   " Then it [the visit of the Magi] is made known to Herod.   Jealously guarding his power he orders the children to be slain and makes a multitude of martyrs." [1]   Sedulius opens the second part of his Nativity hymn, already quoted, thus: " Herod, thou wicked foe, why dost thou fear the coming of Christ? He who confers celestial realms, does not deprive thee of a mortal kingdom." [2]   Little could it have been suspected how familiar these words would one day become, as part of the dialogue for a liturgical drama well-known throughout Europe.   Let it be noted that Herod is the chief figure in the story from the beginning and that the enormity of his guilt increases as the story is taken up by the authors of sequences which were used at the feast.   " Then fired by envy and heated with rage he orders the children to be slain, two years old or younger, throughout Bethlehem of David and also in all the neighboring places."—" What wickedness, what savage madness, what unheard-of cruelty! " [3] " Herod, shaken by deep-seated wrath, suddenly orders the children throughout all the borders of Bethlehem to be sought out and then deprived of life." [4]   Of all the condemnations of Herod, the following is the most striking and dramatic. " Ah! Let the voices of children resound in heavenly strains, singing the measured praises of the Innocents whom this day

[1] *Hymnum dicat turba fratrum, Anal. Hymn.,* LI, p. 264, lines 31-34.

[2] *Hostis Herodes impie,* S.B., stanza 1.

[3] *Pura deum laudet innocentia,* W.T., lines 8, 9, 11.

[4] *Epiphaniam domino canamus gloriosam,* S.M., lines 16-18.

the infant Christ has borne upward to the stars. The crushing madness of Herod's deceit slew them for no fault of theirs, both in Bethlehem and all the neighboring places, two years of age or younger. Herod the king, uneasily fearing the sway of the new-born Christ, is filled with rage and brandishes his weapons with proud hand. He seeks the king of light and heaven with mind disordered, that he may put to death by the javelin him who confers life. When the overclouded heart of the murderer cannot endure the heavenly light, hot with wrath, cruel Herod plots once more that he may destroy the ranks of the guiltless. The evil leader assembles the battalion of his soldiers, he plunges the iron into the limbs of his tender victims." [1] Then follow the ghastly details of the massacre and the lamentations of the victims, which are finally resolved into the angelic strains of welcome to the children in celestial glory.

Herod has thus far been pronounced guilty of envy, wickedness, rage, madness, cruelty, deceit and pride. Chiefly characterized by wrath and envy, he makes clear by his conduct that deceit, cruelty and murder are the natural results of yielding to that anger and jealousy which he felt when circumvented by the Magi. Here we have the first of a series of great sinners whom the medieval church held up for detestation. He is the first persecutor, displaying the excessive cruelty and vindictive rage which came to be the conventional characteristics of the Roman officials, particularly the emperors noted for their zeal in attacking the church, as they are described in hymns. His successors will be met later in the hymns praising the virtues of the martyrs.

It is difficult to realize in modern times the prominence once given to that part of the nativity story which concerns the Innocents. In our day Christian thought dwells more upon the pastoral beauty of the shepherd scene or the adora-

---

[1] *Celsa pueri concrepant melodia*, S.M., lines 1-14.

tion of the Magi. The wrath and cruelty of Herod are
somewhat blurred in the full panorama of the Christmas
narrative. To the people of the Middle Ages, Herod stood
well in the foreground. Many had doubtless seen various
forms of the nativity drama in which the massacre was enacted. " Then let Herod, enraged, speak thus to his soldiers :
' Go! Go, at once with sword in hand! Spare no son for his
tender years. Nay, let every mother weep, her breast bereft
of her child, that I may be avenged for the new-born Child! '
Let the soldiers rush and slay the children whose mothers
thus mourn and lament." Then follow the cries of mourn-
ing and tragic lamentation. Picture the satisfaction of the
spectators as the concluding stage directions for this scene
were carried out. " Afterwards let Herod be consumed by
worms, and falling dead from his throne, let him be received
by demons greatly rejoicing, and let the crown of Herod be
placed upon the head of his son Archelaus." [1]   Thus the
drama attributes to Herod the Great, the punishment of
Herod Agrippa I, who, according to Acts 12 : 23, was " eaten
of worms."

The earliest forms of the nativity plays date from the
eleventh century. In a Compiègne manuscript of the *Offi-
cium Pastorum* there is the nucleus of the slaughter scene.
A Norman version pictures the wrath of Herod. " Already
he is beginning to tear a passion to tatters in the manner that
became traditionally connected with his name." [2]   A second
play, *Stella,* in a Laon version contains the massacre scene,
as does a Freising version, while in a Fleury version one part
of the play is called *Interfectio Puerorum.* Many versions
have the Archelaus incident. [3]   The plaint of Rachel was also

[1] *Ludus scenicus de nativitate domini* in *Carmina Burana, Bibliothek
des Literarischen Vereins in Stuttgart* (Stuttgart: 1847), vol. xvi, p. 91.

[2] E. K. Chambers, *Mediaeval Stage,* II, p. 48.

[3] E. K. Chambers, *ibid.,* II, chap. xix; W. Creizenach, *Geschichte des
Neueren Dramas* (Halle: Niemeyer, 1911), I, p. 57.

employed as a central motive.   In one form of the Rachel
play, embodied in the Freising-Munich text, the hymn *Hostis
Herodes impie* is incorporated.[1]   Essentially universal, the
liturgical dramas possessed a uniformity which was a dis-
tinct advantage in reinforcing the teachings of the church.
As an outgrowth of the liturgy, they are closely related to the
hymns of the season in which they were enacted.   Consequently these hymns assume an unexpected importance, and
in this particular instance, the condemnation of the sin of
wrath through hymn and drama is most effectively conveyed.

Following closely upon the feast of the Holy Innocents is
that of Epiphany, connected with it by the narrative of the
visit of the Magi to the infant Jesus.   In the western church
this aspect of Epiphany was given great prominence.[2]   Fundamentally, the incident illustrates a phase of the relationship
existing between Christ and the church.   The Gentile world
is first brought to the worship of the Christ Child, as the
Magi offer their gifts.   Many other symbolic ideas are connected with Epiphany and its hymns but this will suffice to
show how the virtues are pictured as both an ornament and
an offering of the church.   " She is that queen, adorned with
the golden veil of the virtues, sitting at the right hand of
God, whose glory is from within." [3]   A sequence from the
Hereford missal presents the metaphorical interpretation
which has come to be traditionally associated with the gold,
frankincense and myrrh, and a reinterpretation of the frankincense as the gift of virtues.   " Rejoice, ye faithful, chosen
from the Gentiles!   The darkness of the Ethiopians is
brought to Judah.   The Arabians offer gold, Tarshish and
Sheba frankincense.   Mystically they show forth who He is

[1] P. E. Kretzmann, *Liturgical Element in the Earliest Forms of the
Medieval Drama* (Minneapolis: Bulletin Univ. of Minn., 1916), p. 60.

[2] V. Thalhofer, *Handbuch der Katholischen Liturgik*, I, pp. 680-681.

[3] *Gaude virgo, mater ecclesia*, W.T., lines 9-10.

to whom they bring their gifts; the king, by the gold, the priest by the frankincense, his burial by the myrrh. Let us offer to Christ in reality what the kings brought in the figure. Let us search our hearts and gold is upon the altar, let us mortify ourselves for sin and thus myrrh is offered, while the odor of frankincense, the finest that Sheba has provided, pertains to the gift of the virtues." [1]

Such are the contributions of the hymns of Advent, Nativity and Epiphany to the ethical values of medieval Christianity. The season opens with a summons to amend the faults of life and conduct, and prepare for the judgment to come. It closes with the desire to offer the gift of a virtuous life to God. Specifically the great virtue which has been emphasized is humility, accompanied by faith and hope. The great sins to be avoided are wrath and envy which lead to cruelty, lying and murder.

It is significant that hymns for Lent are so often selected from those vigorous early compositions which exalt the life of courageous activity and of purity in word, thought and action, which may be regarded as the positive aspects of asceticism. Primarily, however, Lent is the season of denial and abstinence, the negative aspects of the ascetic life. They are to be accompanied by sincere repentance and sorrow for wrong-doing. Even in the pre-Lenten period beginning with Septuagesima Sunday, a strong sense of sin is felt. " Now we do not deserve to sing the endless Alleluia. Guilt compels us to interrupt the Alleluia. The time is at hand in which we should mourn the sins we have committed." [2]

Scriptural precedents for the season of fasting and abstinence reach far back into the Old Testament. The very first hymn for Lent in the Sarum breviary makes this clear, at the

---

[1] *Gaudete vos fideles gentium pars electa*, H.M., lines 1-9.
[2] *Alleluia dulce carmen*, D.H., stanza 3.

same time striking the appropriate note for the entire season.
" Taught by mystic custom let us keep this fast, the circle of
ten days, four times repeated. The law and the prophets in
olden days prescribed it and Christ, the king and creator of
the seasons, made it sacred. Therefore let us use more
sparingly, words, food and drink, sleep and jests; let us stand
more strictly on guard." [1] Moses, Elijah, Daniel and John
the Baptist are lauded in another hymn which closes with
these words: " Grant O God, that we may follow their
examples of abstinence. Do thou increase the vigor of our
minds and grant us spiritual joy." [2]

Aside from the precedents to which they point, hymns for
Lent almost always contain phrases which identify them unmistakably with the season. " Hear, beneficent creator, our
prayers and tears poured out in this sacred feast of forty
days.—May we so wear away the flesh through abstinence
that the sober mind may be free from the stain of sins." [3]
" O Jesus, founder of the forty days of abstinence who hast
consecrated this fast for the health of our souls, be present to
restore to paradise by the keeping of the fast, those whom the
enticement of gluttony has driven from it." [4] Disobedience
is usually considered to be the sin of Adam and Eve but they
are accused here of gluttony, by inference, it is true. Another hymn has a clearer reference. " Grant us cleanness of
heart and chastity of life lest the corruptor of purity be able
to attack us, he who, enticing our first parents by forbidden
food, thrust them into the burning prison house of this life." [5]

This is the first time that the mention of gluttony has been

---

[1] *Ex more docti mystico*, S.B., stanzas 1-3.

[2] *Clarum decus jejunii*, S.B., stanza 4.

[3] *Audi benigne conditor*, S.B., stanzas 1, 4.

[4] *Jesu, quadragenariae*, S.B., stanzas 1, 2. The above translation is
made from Walpole's reading, *Early Latin Hymns*, p. 325.

[5] *Summe salvator omnium*, D.H., stanzas 2, 3.

noted, but it is so stressed in thought as to correspond to the fundamental importance given to it by Cassian in his discussion of the eight sins. It is quite natural that the word gluttony should appear rarely in hymns. There is an exceptional case where gluttony is described, which seems to prove most adequately that the idea does not lend itself to poetic treatment in hymnology.[1] As a matter of fact, the sin of gluttony is attacked by the weapon of fasting. Eminently true of teachings in Lenten hymns, the same lesson is effectively conveyed in the praise of saintly examples to be considered later.

Purity of heart and life, so often praised in hymns, is closely associated with Lenten abstinence as the above citations have made plain. The devil has appeared, playing his role of antagonist to man, a familiar idea in hymns for all parts of the liturgical year. As one aspect of spiritual struggle, that is, the idea of allegorical combat between the soul of man and the devil, it corresponds to the method of Prudentius who helped to make this theme so popular in medieval thought. As early as the eighth century a simple form of the allegory is reflected in a hymn for Lent: " But let the mind, like a watchman, supported by the weapons of purity, with sobriety as comrade, repel the base enemy of man." [2]

Several of the hymns for Lent have come to be associated with the name of Gregory the Great.[3] He has also been credited with the authorship of the series of vesper hymns, already mentioned, which are a part of the Anglo-Irish cycle.

[1]   Sed nec ciborum crapula
        Tandem distendat corpora
        Ne vi per somnum animam
        Ludificatam polluat.
            Iam ter quaternis trahitur, Y.B., stanza 4.

[2] *Iam ter quaternis trahitur*, Y.B., stanza 3.

[3] They are *Clarum decus jejunii, Audi benigne conditor, Ecce tempus idoneum* and *Summi largitor praemii. Vide* Julian, p. 470.

The story goes that St. Columba of Iona composed a hymn for Gregory the Great, *Altus Prosator,* in return for the gift of seven hymns with which Gregory had presented him.[1] Frere suggests that, if Gregory is the author of the vesper hymns, his influence may have had something to do with the establishment of the second cycle, and that this may be the explanation of its triumphant course. The authorship of the Lenten, as well as the vesper hymns must remain uncertain but both are perfectly congenial to his thought, particularly the former group. The monastic ideal, already influential, acquired additional prestige when Gregory the Great was called from the monastery to the papal chair (590-604). This great religious leader possessed a vision embracing the needs of Christian and barbarian, of clergy and laity alike throughout the European world as it was known to him. He wished to apply to secular life everywhere in Christendom the same standards which, in monastic life, had commended themselves to him as a supreme moral test. That he succeeded is beyond question, so much so that to his influence may be traced, in part, the medieval conception of the monk as the ideal man. " And if monasticism in the West developed into a mighty force for the leavening of medieval society and the redemption of the medieval church, it was owing in large measure to the wisdom and energy of the first monk-pope." [2]

On the other hand, it should not be assumed that the medieval church expected all its members to enter the cloister. Neither should the lists of sins and virtues so far as they represent a standard of perfection, be confused with the monastic vows of poverty, chastity and obedience, although

---

[1] W. H. Frere, *Hymns Ancient and Modern*, Introd., p. xvii; C. Blume, *Anal. Hymn.*, LI, p. 275 *et seq.*

[2] F. H. Dudden, *Gregory the Great* (London: Longman's, 1905), II, p. 200.

they overlap at certain points.   Rather should the monk or
nun be thought of as an exemplar and teacher of seven great
virtues to which, as Aquinas said in a later period, the whole
of morality might be reduced.[1]   The actual lists of three
theological virtues and four cardinal virtues was not a product of the monastery, as has been shown above.   The lists
of sins, on the contrary, were formed under monastic auspices
and were extended in their application to the lives of laymen.
Important stages in the process of widening their sphere of
influence in this direction will be mentioned below.   On the
whole, it is undoubtedly true that monasticism was a potent
influence in shaping medieval ethical standards, as to their
origin, dissemination or both.

Hymnology in its relation to ethics, may be viewed from a
similar point of view.   The earliest Latin hymns were composed for the laity and were used for some two hundred years
before the hour cycle was established by monastic Rules.
Monasticism conserved and increased the church's store of
hymns, just as it conserved and enlarged the body of its
ethical teachings.   Throughout the medieval period the rites
and activities of the regular clergy had a tendency to pene-
trate into the sphere of the secular clergy and through both
to the laity, in channels too numerous and too familiar to be
mentioned here.   The full cycle of liturgical hymns reflects
therefore, every aspect of the ideal life, whether practiced by
monk or layman.   The monk, it is true, embodies an ideal
which receives the greatest prominence in medieval hymns,
but side by side with him appears the knight, also highly
approved.   For the present, all that may be concluded is this:
The perfections of the ascetic life are presented in the hymns
for Lent; the sins of pride, impurity and intemperance in
food and drink are condemned; the virtues of purity and

---

[1] Aquinas, *Summa*, II, ii, Prologue.

self-control, especially in the form of abstinence, are
approved.

It may be helpful at this point to leave the hymns and return to the consideration of the lists of sins which existed
prior to the pontificate of Gregory the Great, and to trace
the development of the lists under his influence and that of
his successors up to 1100.

This is the period in which the lists of sins and virtues,
made by Cassian and others, take on a legalistic character
and are transformed into a practical guide for the penitential
system of the church. Not only the monk but the layman
becomes subject to the discipline which is suggested by the
standard of the seven sins. Associated with the sacrament
of penance, the seven are all-pervasive, and must needs be
reflected in hymns as well as other forms of religious literature. If their presence is to be traced in hymnology the
nature of contemporary teaching and expression must be
known. It will be recalled that Cassian's list contained eight
principal sins, namely, gluttony, lust, vain glory, pride,
avarice, wrath, melancholy and sloth. Gregory, in his commentary on the Book of Job, expounds the subject of seven
sins, altering both the number and the specific sins in Cassian's list. Like Augustine, Gregory places pride first as the
root of all sins. He introduces envy into the list. He com-
bines the related sins, melancholy and indifference, into one,
that is melancholy, and he places impurity last. Gregory's
list therefore reads: pride, envy, wrath, melancholy, avarice,
gluttony and lust.[1] Up to Gregory's time the lists had
varied and they continued to vary in the centuries immediately
following. But the variations were minor ones. Sloth
(*acedia*), for instance, rivaled melancholy (*tristitia*) in the
nomenclature employed. Cassian's list was kept alive by

---

[1] Gregory the Great, *Moralia*, xxxi, 45.

Alcuin although he reinforced Gregory's attempt to apply the monastic standard to lay morality.[1]

Another influence operating powerfully in the same direction was that of the *Penitentials*. The *Penitentials* offered a scheme of prescribed penalties, upon confession of sin, originally intended for the Celtic monasteries of the sixth and seventh centuries. Finian and Columbanus were among the earliest authors. Theodore of Tarsus (d. 690) and Bede (d. 735) spread the system in Britain. It is essentially a system of private as opposed to public confession and penance practiced by the early church, used first by the monks but from Theodore's time by laymen.[2] Where the decalogue might have been assumed as the church's foundation for a layman's ethics, the lists of Cassian and Gregory are in reality employed. So in the *Penitential* of Egbert (d. 766) and in the *Paris Penitential* Gregory's list appears, while the system of Cassian finds expression in the *Penitential* of Halitgar of Cambrai and in that of Theodore of Tarsus.[3] So widespread was the knowledge of Cassian's eight principal sins that Watkins regards them as a commonplace of clerical training in the ninth century.[4]

During the century another very influential book was produced by Regino, abbot of Prüm (d. 915), at the instance of Ratbod, archbishop of Trier. It was entitled *De ecclesiasticis disciplinis et religione Christiana* and was a work on

[1] Alcuin, *De virtutibus et vitiis ad Widonem* (PL, ci, 613-638) ; *De ratione animae ad Eulaliam* (PL, ci, 639-650).

[2] O. D. Watkins, *History of Penance* (London: Longmans Green & Co., 1920), II, pp. 757-765.

[3] O. Zöckler, *Das Lehrstück von den sieben Hauptsünden*, pp. 57, 58. T. P. Oakley, *English Penitential Discipline* (New York: Col. Univ. Dissertation, 1923), p. 110.

[4] Watkins, *op. cit.*, I, p. 460.

church disciplne for use in ecclesiastical visitations.[1] It contains the topic *Ordo ad dandam poenitentiam* under which eight principal sins are grouped with the evils which accompany them. " Now I will expound to you the eight principal sins, namely, pride, vain glory, envy, wrath, melancholy, avarice, gluttony and impurity. If you perceive that you are guilty of them, do penance, for from these arise all the vices. From pride which is the origin of every sin and the queen of all evil deeds, arises every act of disobedience, audacity, obstinacy; controversies, heresies and arrogance. From vain glory arise disobedience, boasting, hypocrisy, controversies, obstinacy, discords and novel presumptions. From envy arise hatred, gossip, detraction of others, satisfaction in the misfortunes of a neighbor, and grief when he is prosperous. From wrath arise brawlings, fury, scorn, complaint, indignation, blasphemy. From melancholy arises malice, rancor, cowardice, despair, inactivity, wandering of the mind. From avarice arise betrayal, fraud, deceits, perjury, unrest, and a hardening of the heart against pity. From gluttony are produced senseless merriment, scurrility, impurity, loquacity, heaviness of the senses. From impurity there grows mental blindness, lack of consideration, unfaithfulness, rashness, love of self, hatred of God, attachment to the present world, horror and despair in the face of the world to come." [2]

---

[1] Regino, *De Ecclesiasticis Disciplinis et Religione Christiana* (Paris: Muguet, 1671).

[2] *Nunc tibi octo principalia vitia explicabo, id est, superbiam, vanam gloriam, invidiam, iram, tristitiam, avaritiam, ventris ingluviem, luxuriam. Ex quibus si te culpabilem recognoscis, poenitentiam suscipe. Nam ex his omnia vitia oriuntur. De superbia, quae initium omnis peccati est et regina omnium malorum, nascitur omnis inobedientia, omnis praesumptio, et omnis pertinacia, contentiones, haereses, arrogantia. De vana gloria oriuntur inobedientia, jactantia, hypocrisis, contentiones, pertinacia, discordiae, novitatum praesumptiones. De invidia nascitur odium, susurratio, detractio, exultatio in adversis proximi, afflictio in prosperis. De ira oriuntur rixiae, tumor mentis, contumeliae,*

The passage is quoted in full so that prevalent opinion upon the subject as it existed at this period may be better understood. Regino's work was sufficiently important to be used as one of the sources for the *Collectarium Canonum* or *Decretum* compiled by Burchard of Worms (d. 1025), which was used up to the time of Gratian's *Decretum*.[1]

What may be termed the legalistic or juristic treatment of the deadly sins is illustrated in Regino's work. The *Penitentials* already described and the *Summae Confessorum* which will be discussed later, are of a similar nature. All three were written from the standpoint of the canonist rather than of the theologian or moralist.

As one looks back over the period from the pontificate of Gregory the Great to the end of the eleventh century, a strong tendency may be observed to fix the number of deadly sins at seven. The lists that contain eight sins include *superbia* and *vana gloria* which are in reality, two forms of one sin. Variations between *acedia* and *tristitia* point to one concept of which they are different phases. Consequently, it is not surprising that when the twelfth century opened, Peter Lombard should find the lists of sins ready to be crystallized into permanent form.

The hymns of the liturgy beginning with Palm Sunday and ending with Ascension will be considered as one group. The series is exceptionally interesting for several reasons. The primitive cycle of hymns, it will be recalled, was divided

clamor, indignatio, blasphemiae. *De tristitia nascitur malitia, rancor, pusillanimitas, desperatio, torpor, vagatio mentis. De avaritia oriuntur proditio, fraus, fallacia, perjuria, inquietudo, et contra misericordiam obduratio. De ventris ingluvie propagatur inepta laetitia, scurrilitas, immunditia, multiloquium, hebetudo sensus. De luxuria generatur caecitas mentis, inconsideratio, inconstantia, praecipitatio, amor sui, odium Dei, affectus praesentis seculi, horror et desperatio futuri.*

Regino, *op. cit.*, p. 146.

[1] The passage just quoted is *lib.* 19, c. 6 of Burchard's work, as shown on p. 146 of the edition of Regino's book cited above.

into two parts, those for Easter and those for the rest of
the year. Historically, therefore, Easter hymns were the
first to be differentiated. The primitive cycle is represented
here by three hymns; *Aurora lucis rutilat, Ad cenam agni
providi* and *Hic est dies verus dei.* In the Sarum collection,
all the Easter compositions were in existence before 1100,
with the exception of two sequences. Again, the Easter
series includes several of the finest Latin hymns, notably
those of Fortunatus, *Pange lingua gloriosi proelium cer-
taminis* with its continuation, *Lustra sex qui iam peracta* and
Vexilla regis prodeunt, all three for Passion Sunday; and his
Easter processional *Salve festa dies—Qua deus.* The Palm
Sunday processional *Gloria laus et honor,* by Theodulphus of
Orleans,[1] also belongs to this group and, in addition, the
hymn of Prudentius, *O redemptor sume carmen,* and the
resurrection hymn, *Chorus novae Hierusalem,* which has been
attributed to Fulbert of Chartres.[2] Finally, the Easter series
contains the sequence *Victimae paschali laudes* which derives
its importance from its wide use in the liturgical drama.

Easter hymns are not primarily concerned with problems
of conduct. The thoughts of the worshipper are directed
rather to salvation by atonement, to immortality, and to the
praises of the crucified, risen and ascending Christ. Salvation in its other aspect, that is, the reward of struggle with
temptation and sin, has become familiar in hymns already
cited. The idea of spiritual combat, allegorically expressed,
was a feature of at least one Lenten hymn studied. It was
also implicit in every hymn which holds up an ideal to be attained by courage, restraint or denial. It will be amply illustrated in later sections where militant figures of saints and
martyrs are considered. During the Easter season it is sub-
ordinated, with one interesting exception which will be men-

[1] *Vide* Julian, p. 426.
[2] *Vide* Julian, p. 224.

tioned presently. Although conduct is not stressed, there
are many allusions which suggest, sometimes very strikingly,
the abhorrence of certain sins and the aspiration to certain
virtues on the part of the individual. Pride, for instance, is
a characteristic of man's ancient enemy whom Jesus has
overcome.[1] The contrasting virtue of humility is displayed
by Jesus riding into the city of Jerusalem upon an ass, or
washing his disciples' feet.[2] " Rising from the exalted
feast, he sets an example to mortals, because of his humility
approaching the feet of Peter." [3] These two incidents, like
the humble surroundings of Jesus' birth, have always made a
profound impression upon Christian thought. In the Middle
Ages the desire to imitate the life of humility and poverty
led by Jesus upon earth, had a unique social value. Words
like these were connected in the thought of the period with
the chief inspiration of the monastic ideal, with movements
toward church reform and with countless gracious acts of
private life. If there is a value for religious education in
the praise of a loving humility, equal to or greater than that
of the denunciation of the sin of pride, then the hymn writers
of the Middle Ages are justified in this method of attacking
the deadly sins.

The incidents which took place during the Last Supper include the announcement that Judas is about to betray Jesus
to his enemies. " Jesus tells what will come to pass, to his
disciples reclining at the feast; ' One of you will betray me.'
Judas, basest of traffickers, seeks his master with a kiss which
He, guiltless as the sacrificial lamb, does not refuse. Christ
is handed over to the Jews for a price; guiltless and sinless is
He whom the wicked Judas betrays." [4] The act by which

[1] *Fulgens praeclara rutilat*, S.M., line 2.

[2] *Magnum salutis gaudium*, Anal. Hymn., LI, no. 74, stanzas 6, 7.

[3] *Tellus ac aether jubilant*, D.H., stanza 3. Cf. *Laudes salvatori voce
modulemur*, S.M., line 9.

[4] *Hymnum canamus domino*, Anal. Hymn., LI, no. 75, stanzas 3-5.

Judas sold his Master for thirty pieces of silver made him the prototype of the sin of avarice. Thereafter, he stood out, like Herod, among the great sinners of the Christian narrative.

Beyond the limits of hymnology, churchmen themselves did not hesitate to condemn the sin of avarice among their own representatives by reference to the act of Judas, as a large number of poems in the *Carmina Burana* bears witness. Avarice is denounced in student songs in terms of the most trenchant satire. Among several poems chosen at random from the Benedictbeuern collection, perhaps the most forceful condemnation of the sin of Judas is the following: "Judas deserved the penalties of hell because he, on one occasion only, sold Christ. But tell me, ye who seven times daily sell the body of the Lord, what shall be your punishment?"[1]

Faith and hope are quickened by the Easter season. Both are prominent in the hymns. "Thou dost crush the strength of the ancient enemy through the death of the cross, just as we, marked with that sign upon our foreheads, bear the ensign of faith."[2] "He has granted us in his mercy a strong hope that we may hereafter rise to eternity."[3] "He has ascended into the clouds and has given hope to believers, opening paradise which our first parents had closed."[4]

Faith and hope are closely connected in the Easter series with redemption. The word *iustus* is employed to mean the "redeemed" or "justified," and *iustitia* to indicate "re-

---

[1] *Judas gehennam meruit, Carmina Burana*, p. 42 (edition cited above) stanza 1. Other poems in the collection condemning avarice are: *De ammonitione praelatorum*, stanza 7, pp. 10, 11; *Propter Sion non tacebo*, stanza 4, p. 16; *Utar contra vitia*, stanza 12, p. 20; *Ecce torpet probitas*, stanza 2, p. 37; *Flete flenda*, stanza 3, p. 38; *Versus de nummo*, p. 43; *Artifex qui condidit*, stanza 4, p. 76.

[2] *Rex aeterne domine*, D.H., stanza 10.

[3] *Jubilans concrepa nunc paraphonista*, W.T., lines 7-9.

[4] *Optatus votis omnium*, D.H., stanza 4.

demption " or " justification." Confusion at once arises as
to the relation, if any, with the words *iustus* meaning " just "
and *iustitia* meaning " justice." Since justice is one of the
four cardinal virtues and, as such, an important attribute of
the ideal Christian life in the opinion of medieval teachers,
it is necessary to study the passages containing the words
iustus and *iustitia* a little more intensively. The just man
would seem to correspond most closely with the righteous
man of the Scriptures and justice with righteousness, in the
sense of the cardinal virtue. On the other hand, many passages must be interpreted similarly to those in Easter hymns.

Perhaps the most satisfactory way to clear up the difficulty
is to consider what the theologians had to say about *iustus*
and *iustitia*. Two streams of thought mingled in their opinions. The former, derived from the Old Testament, presented the just man as one who had fulfilled completely his
obligations to the Jewish law; and justice itself, as a divine
characteristic. The latter, derived from Aristotle, presented
the just man as one who rendered to another his due; and
justice as a social virtue directed toward that end. Justification is a divine work which Aquinas defines thus; *Justificatio
importat transmutationem quandam de statu injustitiae, ad
statum justitiae praedictae, per remissionem peccati.*[1] Justice
as related to conduct is treated at great length by Aquinas,
in all its implications. This is, of course, the aspect which is
most pertinent to the present study.[2]

The confusion which has been observed in the use of the
terms *iustus* and *iustitia* in hymns is not one of ideas but of
words. In most cases the context is clear and the various
meanings can be determined easily. Justice is a divine
characteristic. "Now, O Christ, sun of justice [or righteous-

---

[1] *Vide Dictionnaire de Théologie catholique*, " Justification ". *Vide*
Schutz, *Thomas-Lexicon* (Paderborn: Schöningh, 1895), *Justificatio.*

[2] Aquinas, *Summa Theologica*, II, ii, 57-79.

ness] let the darkness of the mind clear away, that the light of the virtues may return while thou dost restore day to the earth." [1]   The penitent thief is justified. " Whom does the pardon of the thief not free from the burden of fear? Who, changing his cross into his reward, sought Jesus by a moment of faith and, justified, entered first into the kingdom of God." [2] The just or righteous are rewarded in the final judgment as Advent hymns made clear.[3] No hymn, however, so closely expresses the conception of justice, as it approaches the meaning of grace requisite for redemption, as *Vexilla regis prodeunt,* one of the outstanding compositions of the Middle Ages in the field of religious literature. "Hail, O cross, our only hope, at this passion-tide, increase justification to the holy and grant pardon to sinners." [4]

As the subject of justice in human relationships will be expanded later, the presentation of ideals found in hymns of the Easter series will be concluded with a brief mention of the militant attitude which is revealed in *Chorus novae Hierusalem.* Here the spirit of the hymn seems to indicate that the knightly ideal is present to the writer's mind. The hymn is found in at least two manuscripts of the eleventh century,[5]

[1]   Iam Christe sol iustitiae
         Mentis diescant tenebrae
         Virtutum ut lux redeat
         Terris diem dum reparas. D.H., stanza 1.

[2]   Qui praemium mutans cruce
         Jesum brevi quaesiit fide
         Iustusque praevio gradu
         Pervenit in regnum dei.
  Hic est dies verus dei, Anal. Hymn., L, no. 12, lines 7-12.

[3] *Verbum supernum prodiens,* S.B., lines 11, 12.

[4]   O crux ave spes unica
         Hoc passionis tempore,
         Auge piis justitiam
         Reisque dona veniam.
         Vexilla regis prodeunt, S.B., stanza 7.

[5] Julian, p. 224.

a period which Henry Adams believed to have been dominated by a militant ideal which is typified by St. Michael in heaven and the lusty knights of the *Chansons de Geste* upon earth.[1] It would seem most natural that knighthood and chivalry in their ideal aspects would find their way into the hymnology of the age, as soon as they became influential in social life. The spiritual warrior of *Chorus novae Hierusalem* appears in the guise of knighthood. In the opening stanzas the Paschal victory is recounted. Two closing stanzas depict the knights of the faith acclaiming the victory of their royal Leader, as they hope one day to be assembled in some feudal hall of the heavenly country. " He triumphs gloriously and, worthy of all dignity, he unites the realm of earth and heaven into one kingdom. In our hymns, let us, suppliant knights, implore our king himself to assemble our ranks in his most glorious palace." [2]

The relation between Ascension and Pentecost is close and immediate. " He commanded them not to depart from Jerusalem but to await the promised gifts; ' For not many days hence I will send to you the Spirit, the Paraclete upon earth '." [3] These words from a sequence for Ascension have their counterpart in one for Pentecost. " The phalanx of the apostles, gathered together in one place, awaited the heralded gifts." [4] The word *munera* which is used in these passages cannot be interpreted as a plural used poetically for the singular to mean the gift of the Holy Spirit himself, for

[1] H. Adams, *Mont-Saint-Michel and Chartres* (Boston and N. Y.: Houghton Mifflin Co., 1913), chaps. i-iii.

[2]   Triumphat ille splendide   Ipsum canendo supplices
         Et dignus amplitudine,   Regem precemur milites,
         Soli polique patriam,   Ut in suo clarissimo
         Unam facit rempublicam.   Nos ordinet palatio.
                    Chorus novae Hierusalem, S.B., stanzas 4, 5.

[3] *Rex omnipotens, die hodierna*, S.M., lines 10-12.

[4] *Resonet sacrata iam turma*, S.M., line 3.

other hymns clearly distinguish between the Holy Spirit and the gifts. " He pours into the hearts of men the riches of deity, proceeding from the Father bearing mystic gifts." [1] " May he (*Paraclitus*) pour into our hearts the gifts of his anointing that our life may be pleasing to him forever." [2] " Now, O God most merciful, we beseech thee with heads bent low, to grant us the gifts of the Spirit, fallen from heaven." [3] Finally, the hymns afforded a clear reference to the number of the gifts. " Thou with sevenfold gift, the forefinger of the right hand of God." [4] A phrase like this implies familiarity with the Old Testament teaching upon which the idea is based. The seven gifts are emunerated in Isaiah 11 :2, 3, as follows : " And the spirit of the Lord shall rest upon him : the spirit of wisdom, and of understanding, the spirit of counsel, and of fortitude, the spirit of knowledge and of godliness. And he shall be filled with the spirit of the fear of the Lord." [5] Two of the seven gifts, wisdom and fortitude, are also two of the four cardinal virtues, and in this resemblance lies the only literal connection between the seven gifts and the seven virtues as they had grouped themselves in medieval thought. But the symbolic treatment of the ideas was to result in the welding of the four cardinal virtues and the three theological virtues, hitherto appearing side by side but not unified into a single concept. Before tracing the symbolic relationships between the gifts and the virtues as they are found in medieval religious literature, another feature of the Pentecostal hymns should be explained. The Holy Spirit is thought of as a

[1] *Salve festa dies . . . Qua deus*, Y.P., lines 5, 6.

[2] *Laudes deo devota dulci voce*, S.M., lines 8-11.

[3] *Beata nobis gaudia*, S.B., stanza 5.

[4] *Veni creator spiritus*, S.B., lines 9, 10.

[5] Douay version. In the Vulgate the Latin terms are : *sapientia, intellectus, consilium, fortitudo, scientia, pietas* and *timor domini*.

powerful purifying force. " May the grace of the Holy
Spirit be present with us, to make our hearts his own habita-
tion, after all the vices of the soul have been driven out.—
Thou Spirit, purifier of all our shameful acts, cleanse the
eye of the inner man that we may behold the supreme creator." [1] " Do thou cleanse us from our sins, thyself the
author of purity." [2] " Gracious Spirit, cleanse us from our
sins ; adorn us with the flower of the virtues." [3]

A third feature of the hymns for Pentecost, which has
been observed in those used at terce, is the prominence given
to the virtue of love. In itself, the exaltation of love as a
virtue implies all the rest, for Augustine, it will be recalled,
had taught that love was the source of all the virtues. " Pour
love into our hearts." [4] " The flame with its flickering light,
symbolized the tongue, that they might be eloquent in speech
and glowing with love." [5] " Grant us love that is true and
the manifold gifts of love." [6] Perhaps the idea of purifica-
tion and love accompanying the descent of the Holy Spirit
helped to strengthen the connection between gifts and virtues,
the consideration of which must be resumed at this point.

Ambrose had called the seven gifts virtues.[7] Gregory the
Great asserted that they formed the four cardinal virtues
and were themselves opposed to contracting sins.[8] Isidore
of Seville (d. 636) thought of the gifts as freeing men from
the domination of sins, but neither Gregory nor Isidore
established a permanent relation between the four cardinal

[1] *Sancti spiritus assit nobis gratia*, S.B., lines 1-3, 8-10.
[2] *Lux iocunda lux insignis*, S.M., lines 37, 38.
[3] *Gaude mater ecclesia*, W.T., line 13.
[4] *Veni creator spiritus*, S.B., line 14.
[5] *Beata nobis gaudia*, S.B., stanza 2.
[6] *Veni spiritus aeternorum alme*, H.M., line 8.
[7] Ambrose, *De sacramentis*, iii, 2, 8 (PL, xvi, 434).
[8] Gregory the Great, *Moralia*, i, 27 (PL, lxxv, 544).

virtues and the three theological virtues.[1] It was Hugh of
St. Victor (d. 1141), who finally gave perfect expression to
the teaching that the seven gifts were the source of the seven
virtues and that they in turn, were opposed to the seven sins.
" Over against these seven sins are the virtues which the
seven gifts of the Holy Spirit bring forth. Between the
gifts, however, and the virtues, there is this difference,
namely, that the gifts are the primary impulses in the heart,
certain seeds, as it were, of the virtues, sowed over the field
of our heart. The virtues are like the crops which spring
up from them." [2]

When Bonaventura wrote his commentary on Peter Lombard's *Sententiae* he further explained the mutual relationship of gifts, virtues and sins as follows:

Gifts	Virtues	Sins
wisdom	love	impurity
understanding	faith	gluttony
counsel	hope	avarice
fortitude	fortitude	sloth
knowledge	prudence	wrath
godliness	justice	envy
fear of the Lord	self-control	pride [3]

Citations have twice been made from *Veni creator spiritus*,
perhaps the greatest medieval hymn ever written in celebration of the Holy Spirit. Walpole says of this hymn, which
appeared about the tenth century: " No other Latin hymn,
except those of the daily offices has been so frequently and
widely used as this." [4] It is one of those rare hymns whose
strains were occasionally heard beyond the walls of church or
monastery, carrying the spirit of worship even into warfare.

[1] Isidore, *Sententiae*, ii, 37 (PL, lxxxiii, 638).
[2] Hugh of St. Victor, *Summa sententiarum*, iii, 17 (PL, clxxvi, 114).
[3] Bonaventura, *Opera Omnia* (Florence: Quaracchi, 1887) iii, 744-745.
[4] A. S. Walpole, *Early Latin Hymns*, p. 375.

Says Joinville, recounting the departure of Louis IX for the Crusades, 1248, " When the priests and clerks embarked, the captain made them mount to the castle of the ship, and chant psalms in praise of God, that he might be pleased to grant us a prosperous voyage.   They all, with a loud voice, sang the beautiful hymn of *Veni Creator* from the beginning to the end: and while they were singing, the mariners set their sails in the name of God." [1]   It was also heard in the campaigns of Joan of Arc.   " The day we quitted Blois to go to Orleans," says her confessor Pasquerel, " Joan had all the priests assembled.   The banner at their head, they opened the march.   The soldiers followed.   The cortège left the city by the side of the Solonge, chanting *Veni Creator Spiritus* and several other anthems." [2]   In consideration of the wide acquaintance with *Veni creator spiritus* no further evidence from hymns would be required to demonstrate the importance of the contribution which Pentecostal hymns have made to the medieval conception of the ideal life.   The seven gifts, the purifying power, the love which the spirit kindles, are all contained within this one piece.   Its only rival is the " golden sequence ", *Veni sancte spiritus,* which will be quoted in full as the complete. expression of the relation of the Holy Spirit to the life of virtue.

> Veni, sancte spiritus,
> Et emitte coelitus
> Lucis tuae radium :
> Veni, pater pauperum,
> Veni, dator munerum,
> Veni, lumen cordium.

[1] Translation from *Chronicles of the Crusades* (London: Bell & Daldy, 1865), p. 383.

[2] A. B. Paine, *Joan of Arc* (N. Y.: Macmillan Co., 1925), I, p. 133.

Consolator optime,
Dulcis hospes animae,
Dulce refrigerium:
In labore requies,
In aestu temperies,
In fletu solatium.

O lux beatissima,
Reple cordis intima
Tuorum fidelium:
Sine tuo numine
Nihil est in lumine,
Nihil est innoxium.

Lava quod est sordidum,
Riga quod est aridum,
Sana quod est saucium,
Flecte quod est rigidum,
Fove quod est frigidum,
Rege quod est devium.

Da tuis fidelibus,
In te confidentibus,
Sacrum septenarium.
Da virtutis meritum,
Da salutis exitum
Da perenne gaudium.[1]   S.M.

The feasts of the Proper of the Season as found in

[1] 1. "Come, Holy Spirit, send down from heaven the radiance of thy light. Come, father of the needy, giver of gifts, illumination of all hearts. 2. Best comforter, gentle guest of the soul, refreshing sweetness, rest in toil, coolness in heat and solace in tears. 3. O light most blessed, fill the deep places of the hearts of thy faithful followers. Without thy power there is no illumination, no innocence. 4. Cleanse what is unclean, water what is parched, cure what is wounded, bend what is rigid, warm what is cool, direct what has strayed. 5. Grant to thy faithful ones who trust in thee, the sacred sevenfold gifts. Grant the merit of virtue, a death secure, and eternal joy."

the Sarum breviary come to an end with Trinity, Corpus Christi and, although it is not seasonal, Dedication of a Church.[1]   Like the Easter festivals they concentrate the attention of the worshipper upon mysteries of the faith. The first is devoted to the adoration of the Triune God, the second celebrates the mystery of transubstantiation and the third exalts the mystic union of Christ and the church.   For the individual believer, however, the necessity remains, to approach the feast in an attitude of heart and mind which requires the cultivation of purity, faith and hope.   Perhaps this is the ultimate reason in Christian thought for the practice of certain virtues.   Repeatedly the idea has been stressed in hymns already cited, that only the pure in heart shall see God, and that purity is a condition of acceptable worship.[2]   Here we learn that faith and hope must supplement the human reason if the divine mysteries are to be apprehended.   " Let the mind soberly raise itself to God.   May the grace of the Father, Son and Holy Spirit reveal to us the sacred mysteries." [3]   " Let faith arise and hope increase that thus the vision of the true light may be clear to us.   Let us lift up our minds in hope and remain in the true harmony of faith." [4]   Such are the expressions of Trinity hymns.   The same ideas stand out clearly in hymns for Corpus Christi. " Let the flesh be pure, let the heart be clean." [5]   " What thou dost not receive, what thou dost not see, a lively faith confirms, beyond the natural order." [6]   The finest of the

[1] The office for the Feast of Corpus Christi was drawn up by Aquinas at the request of Pope Urban IV, 1263. It belongs to the group of later feasts but will be included here because of its position in the breviary.

[2] Other citations: *Nostra tuba nunc tua*, W.T., line 2; *Angelicae turmae pulcherrima*, W.T., lines 17-20.

[3] *Trinitatem simplicem*, Y.M., lines 6-9.

[4] *Adoremus unitatem*, Y.M., stanzas 8, 9.

[5] *Salve festa dies ... Qua caro*, S.P., line 29.

[6] *Lauda Sion salvatorem*, S.M., stanza 6.

Corpus Christi series, often attributed to Aquinas, is *Pange lingua gloriosi corporis mysterium.* Here the writer has achieved a perfect blending of dogma and mystic fervor revealing faith in that ideal sense which the author of the Epistle to the Hebrews had defined. "Now faith is assurance of things hoped for, a conviction of things not seen" (Hebrews 11:1.). "The Word made flesh causes the real bread to become his flesh by a word. The wine becomes the blood of Christ. Although the sense fails, faith alone suffices to confirm the devoted heart. Let us therefore adore so great a sacrament, and let the ancient law give place to a new rite. Let faith stand forth to supply the weakness of the senses." [1]

Faith is a requisite in maintaining the perpetual bond between Christ and his church.[2] Faith will reveal Christ to the church. "Contemplate thy bridegroom. True faith reveals him whom the letter hides." [3] Faith is also the gift of the church through baptism.[4]

The best known hymn in the group written for the praises of the church is *Hierusalem et Sion filiae,* credited to Adam of St. Victor. Here the grace of love is conceived as flowing from the church amid the rejoicing of angels over the rewards granted to the righteous.[5] The York missal contains a sequence which treats the subject of dedication in a somewhat unconventional manner. Solomon's temple, an Old Testament type of the church, is described as a structure built up of virtues. Chastity, courage and constancy are parts of it, but the length, breadth and height of the temple are faith, hope and love.[6] In this curious little passage the

---

[1] *Pange lingua gloriosi corporis mysterium,* S.B., stanzas 4, 5.
[2] *Salve festa dies . . . Qua sponso,* S.P., lines 7, 8.
[3] *Laetabundus exsultet fidelis,* S.M., lines 14-16.
[4] *Salve festa dies . . . Qua sponso,* S.P., lines 11, 12.
[5] *Hierusalem et Sion filiae,* S.M., verse 14.
[6] *Rex Salomon fecit templum,* Y.M., lines 10-16.

theological virtues receive the prominence which they invariably do in festivals such as the three which are grouped in this section.   Faults of character and conduct have received scant attention in the hymns of this period of the liturgical year, except by implication.   The explanation seems obvious, depending as it does upon the positive attitude toward the virtues.   But in the midst of a Corpus Christi hymn, the theme of spiritual combat occurs, exceptional too, in a connotation which suggests salvation through the atoning sacrifice.   " O thou salvation-bringing sacrifice who dost open the gates of heaven, we are hard pressed by hostile strife.   Grant us strength!   Bear aid! " [1]   It points to the fully developed idea of spiritual warfare, already foreshadowed, and yet to be exemplified in the saints,—an idea depending partly upon the theme of Christian combat which Prudentius had allegorized for the Middle Ages and partly upon the knightly ideal.   Both phases were no doubt connected ultimately with the thought of the Christian warrior which Paul had developed in his Epistle to the Ephesians.

The reality of spiritual warfare depends to a great extent upon the consciousness that sin and evil are actual forces in human experience which must be faced and overcome; in a word, upon the sense of sin itself.   In the York missal there is a sequence for the eleventh Sunday after the Octave of Pentecost, revealing that sense of sin which pervades the entire liturgy.   It is a poetical version of the parable of the Pharisee and the Publican, which occurs in the Gospel for the day.[2]   " He who had committed a multitude of shameful deeds, standing at a distance and meditating upon his sins, was unwilling to raise his eyes to the lofty stars of heaven; but beating his breast, he prayed thus with tears: ' O God,

---

[1] *Verbum supernum prodiens*
  Nec patris linquens dexteram, S.B., stanza 5.

[2] York Missal, I, p. 232.

be merciful to me a sinner and, in thy clemency, destroy all my evil acts.' With this prayer he merited the divine mercy and returned, justified, to his house. Let us, following his example acceptable to God, cry out 'O God, graciously take pity upon us, mercifully forgive us our debts and justify us.' " [1]

Nowhere in the entire range of medieval hymnology is the sense of human sin and unworthiness, the dread of judgment and the hope of divine salvation, so vividly revealed as in the *Dies Irae*. It does not, strictly speaking, belong in this place but it should be mentioned when the subject of the sense of sin is uppermost. There could be no more fitting close to the series of hymns belonging to the Proper of the Season, since with the thought of judgment for sin, the worshipper is once more brought face to face with the teachings made prominent in Advent. Perhaps the greatest Latin poem of the religious literature of the Middle Ages, the *Dies Irae* cannot be quoted in part without destroying the intensity of its poetic and emotional force. In sharp relief against the stormy terrors of the Judgment day, the sinner pleads for mercy in words made familiar to English readers by a multitude of translations. [2]

[1] *Stans a longe*, Y.M.
This ancient sequence, found as early as the tenth century, was widely known in two versions, almost identical in form. *Vide Anal. Hymn.*, LIII, no. 93, 93a. The second version appears in a thirteenth-century manuscript of the Sarum missal and in the Winchester Troper, 305.

[2] The four stanzas following have been selected as illustrative of the general spirit of the poem.

> 12. Ingemisco tanquam reus,
>   Culpa rubet vultus meus;
>   Supplicanti parce, Deus.

> 13. Qui Mariam absolvisti,
>   Et latronem exaudisti;
>   Mihi quoque spem dedisti.

Looking back over the hymns which accompany the services for the Proper of the Season, a very definite ideal of Christian living is seen to emerge. The hymns for the various parts of the year have made their contributions to the ideal but in no one place has it appeared in a complete form. There has been, also, an evolution in the ideal from its earliest aspects to later manifestations. From the point of view of contributions to an ideal, the entire series may be thought of as a cross section which reveals the ethical concepts associated with the liturgical season through its major feasts, apart from the celebrations for the saints. The hymns for the canonical hours stress the importance of self-control and purity, the value of courageous activity and vigilance accompanied by the crowning virtues of faith, hope and love. The same hymns condemn impurity and excess, indifference and sloth, pride, boasting and strife. Such lists of sins and virtues as one may derive from them are indeterminate, and in this regard consistent with the teachings of contemporary religious leaders who instructed the faithful Christian as to good and evil acts. The Advent season brings to mind the judgment and the necessity of a virtuous life in preparation for that event, especially the cultivation of humility, faith and hope. Wrath and envy, so these hymns declare, are destructive to the Christian ideal, leading as they do to cruelty, lies and murder. Lenten hymns offer one of the most distinctive contributions in the entire group for the Proper of the Season. Monastic asceticism leaves its impress at this point in placing such high value upon abstinence, and

16.   Confutatis maledictis,
Flammis acribus addictis,
Voca me cum benedictis.

17.   Oro supplex et acclinis,
Cor contritum quasi cinis,
Gere curam mei finis.

the seal of its disapproval upon pride and intemperance. Here again, purity and impurity are contrasted, as indeed they are in every part of the hymnal. A most interesting phase of the influence exerted upon the development of the Christian church by monastic leaders is here apparent, as the virtues of the conventual life which they commend are brought out in hymns, while the evils to which monasticism was prone are made correspondingly clear. Easter hymns call to mind the beauty of humility, faith and hope, and the hatefulness of pride and avarice. Justice in the sense of righteousness is lauded and the militant ideal receives recognition. Pentecost is a season rich in associations with medieval concepts of virtue, particularly the idea of the seven gifts, the sources of all virtue. Love, the greatest of the virtues, with its purifying power, is made prominent at this time. Hymns for the closing feasts of the year, including Trinity, Corpus Christi and Dedication, teach the value of the theological virtues as a prerequisite to the comprehension of divine mysteries.

Throughout the hymns for the Proper of the Season a strong sense of sin is manifest and the hatred for sin is greatly emphasized. The sins which are most detested are impurity, sloth, pride, wrath and gluttony, all in various forms. Cruelty, deceit and envy have appeared but rarely. Herod and Judas, prototypes of the persecutor and of the avaricious man, have been held up for scorn. On the side of the virtues, the most approved characteristics are purity, fortitude, faith, hope and love. Justice has been less emphasized but the praise of humility has been conspicuous. The close connection between the seven gifts and the virtues has been made clear.

From the point of view of the evolution of the ideal the earliest hymns have reflected certain of the old pagan virtues, namely courage, moderation, justice and prudence, combined

with the Christian trilogy of faith, hope and love.   In this
aspect the work of Ambrose is significant, since the recon-
ciliation of what was best in the old order with the new, constitutes his distinctive contribution.   Under the influence of
monastic prestige various forms of asceticism have gained
approval and in general the ideals of life fostered by monasticism have been extended to the layman.   In this phase of
development the work of such men as Gregory the Great is
evident.   Toward the close of the period ending with 1100,
the knight appears in hymns as an approved type of Christian
warrior, about to take his place in the symbolic struggle
between good and evil already familiar in Christian
allegory.

It must not be forgotten that the hymns for the Proper of
the Season are incomplete without those for the other sections
of the liturgy.   Only a partial revelation of the ethical teachings offered by hymns has been made thus far, and the outlines are still indistinct.   After considering the hymns for
the Common of Saints the summary will be continued and
then brought to a conclusion with the hymns for the Proper
of Saints.

CHAPTER IV

HYMNS FOR THE COMMON OF SAINTS

THE Common of Saints is devoted to the general praises of apostles, martyrs, confessors and virgins. The actual persons whom the worshipper had in mind, are of course, clear. The twelve apostles with St. Paul; the men and women who, like St. Laurence or St. Katherine, lost their lives in the Roman persecutions; and those who, although they did not suffer martyrdom, merited the reward of the saint by virtue of a holy life. All the hymns in the Sarum breviary for the Common of Saints were written by the tenth century, while the York breviary contains *Aeterna Christi munera,* a martyr hymn from the primitive cycle. Many of the sequences in the various liturgies are also representative of the period before 1100.

It has been remarked already that in the eleventh century the same saints, in general, were venerated throughout the Christian west and that when local cults appeared, the hymnal kept pace with their development. England, however, produced relatively few hymns in honor of local saints but used those in the Common of Saints for special feasts. Consequently the group of hymns and sequences devoted to this purpose in England is of special interest, because they are used over and over again and their teachings thus emphasized. Moreover they represent a period of hymn writing which produced a very high standard of literary and religious expression, while the multitude of special compositions honoring saints in the later centuries represent a period of deterioration in hymnology. The choice of these hymns by English liturgists, in place of newer and inferior composi-

115

tions, is evidence of discrimination which was apparently not so strongly felt in other parts of Europe.

They are significant, also, because they introduce the teaching of great principles of conduct through example. It is the more effective, of course, when the individual saint is named or when the saint is held up as an example of a special virtue. Such instances will be presented later. In the group of hymns now being considered, the individuals are thought of as possessing all the virtues [1] or, when differentiated, they appear in the four classifications stated above, the members of each group being the exponents of a particular virtue. It will clarify the treatment of the subject to retain the four divisions, namely, apostles, martyrs, confessors and virgins.

The apostles have the power to inspire men to virtuous lives. " Restore us to the health of right living, bringing us back to the virtues." [2]   They are themselves the conspicuous possessors of prudence, courage and justice. " Be ye therefore, wise (prudent) as serpents; be ye harmless as doves." [3] This is a paraphrase of Matthew 10: 16 which is a part of the apostolic commission. The Latin version runs as follows: *Estote ergo prudentes sicut serpentes et simplices sicut columbae.* The familiar translation of *prudentes* by the word *wise* unfortunately veils the original for English readers. Courage is a necessary accompaniment of the life of Christian warriors among whom the apostles stand out as leaders. " Illustrious warriors " [4] they are called in one place. Another hymn praises them as " Princes of the churches, victorious leaders in warfare, warriors of the heavenly court and true lights of the world ".[5]

[1] *Organicis canamus*, S.B., line 3.
[2] *Exultet caelum laudibus*, S.B., lines 15-16.
[3] *Caeli enarrant gloriam dei*, Y.M., lines 12, 13.
[4] *Clare sanctorum senatus apostolorum*, S.M., line 10.
[5] *Aeterna Christi munera*, Y.B., stanza 2.

Justice is the peculiar attribute of the apostles in their capacity as judges in the world to come. " Ye just judges of the ages." [1] " Lo, the east and the west, the uttermost parts of the earth rejoice that they have you as fathers and await you as judges." [2] " These are magistrates in the heavenly court of the great king." [3] " Twelve judges . . . gather together those scattered throughout the earth." [4] Individual apostles are singled out as follows in hymns which, for convenience, will be included here. St. Peter and St. Paul are named " Judges of the world." [5] Again, they are mentioned thus: " And high above the stars, illustrious in victory, they are magistrates in the court of heaven." [6] It is said of St. Peter, " In the end of the world he will be a judge of the earth." [7] St. Andrew is one " Who by the victory of the apostles prevails in the court of heaven." [8] The belief which is reflected in passages like the above, is founded upon the words of Jesus. " Ye also shall sit upon twelve thrones, judging the twelve tribes of Israel " (Matt. 19: 28). St. Paul, not being included among the original twelve apostles, is, however, considered worthy of like honor by St. Augustine, who quotes St. Paul's words to the Corinthians to support his conviction. " Know ye not that we shall judge angels? " (Cor. 6: 3).[9] In view of their function as judges, therefore, the attribution of justice to the apostles is most natural.

[1] *Exultet caelum laudibus*, S.B., line 5.

[2] *Clare sanctorum senatus apostolorum*, S.B., lines 11-13.

[3] *Alleluia nunc decantet*, S.M., line 21.

[4] *Caeli enarrant gloriam dei*, Y.M., line 19.

[5] *Aurea luce et decore roseo*, S.B., line 6.

[6] *Laude jocunda melos turma*, S.M., stanza 4.

[7] *Felix per omnes festum*, Y.B., line 25.

[8] *Clara cantemus sonoriter*, W.T., line 2.

[9] Augustine, *De civitate Dei*, xx, 5 (PL, xli, 663 or CSEL, xl, 2, 433).

There is a formality about this conception of justice, however, which removes it from ordinary life relationships in
which one individual renders to another his due. The
office of the apostles is made more prominent than the virtue
which accompanies it. Similarly, the use of the word
justice in the sense of Old Testament *righteousness,* already
mentioned, obscures by its general character the application
which the old Greek philosophers associated with the word.
For the above reasons, the treatment of justice in hymns is
a partial presentation. In a later chapter, instances will
be given of saints other than apostles, who are praised for
justice. Here again, the virtue is restricted to men who
occupied stations of responsibility which involved judicial
functions or ability. Possibly the strength of the tradition
as it affected the apostles caused the virtue to be treated in
the same conventional manner when attributed to other saints.
A further restriction in the meaning and application of the
quality of justice as reflected in hymns, points to the same
conclusion, for justice is the only cardinal virtue which is
not associated with women saints.

The hymn writers were evidently thinking of two important phases of the subject of justice, both biblical, in their
poems, the Old Testament conception of righteousness, and
the New Testament conception of justice in the apostolic
court of heaven. A third conception, that of social justice,
which they might have derived from the Old Testament
prophets or from the teachings of Jesus, is lacking in the
English hymns. Since the modern student is apt to be in-
terested, primarily, in social justice as an ethical factor, the
reader of medieval hymns is likely to be disappointed in
their partial presentation of this ideal.

Martyrs receive high praise in hymns for a variety of
virtues, particularly faith, self-control, and above all, courage. The faith of martyrs is made the subject of an ancient

sequence appearing in all three liturgies, Sarum, York and Hereford. The composition is unusual because of the use of musical figures throughout. The word *fides* meaning " faith " and *fides* meaning " strings of a lyre " are inter-woven to express the idea of faith as an inspiration to all the virtues and the essential note in the harmony of the Christian life.[1]

The oldest martyr hymn in existence is *Aeterna Christi munera,* five stanzas of which are found in the York breviary as follows: [2] " Joyfully let us sing the eternal gifts of Christ and the victories of the martyrs, chanting the praises due unto them. Conquering the terror of the world and spurning the pains of the body, by the gain of a holy death, they possess a life of bliss. The martyrs are given over to the flames, and to the teeth of wild beasts. The hand of the raging per-secutor, armed with iron hooks, indulges its fury. Their en-trails hang exposed, their holy blood is poured out, but by the grace of eternal life they remain unmoved. Now, O Re-deemer, we pray thee that thou wouldst unite us, thy lowly servants, to the company of the martyrs for ever and ever."

It will be noted that the persecutor here is guilty of that same mad fury which characterized Herod in the slaughter of the Innocents. Further illustrations of this point occur in hymns to be mentioned later, written in honor of special saints. Renunciation and fortitude are the chief virtues of the martyr as seen in the above hymn, although the former is not greatly emphasized. It comes out more clearly in the following: " Truly did he, justly esteeming as perishable the joys of the world and its harmful flatteries, enter into celes-tial life. Bravely he ran to meet sufferings and endured them manfully; pouring out his blood for thee, he gains eternal rewards." [3] All three virtues of faith, renunciation,

[1] *Organicis canamus,* S.B.
[2] Walpole, p. 104.
[3] *Deus tuorum militum,* S.B., stanzas 2, 3.

and courage are prominent in the next citation. " They are the warriors who fought the wars of the world. As saints with white crowns, they are crowned who believed, fitly making their confession or, striving by faith, renounced vanities." [1] The note of triumph in one of the Sarum hymns is combined with a prayer to be roused from sin and indifference. " O martyr of God, who by following the only Son of the Father triumphs over conquered enemies and enjoys as victor the celestial rewards, do thou, interceding by virtue of the gift of thyself, wash away our sin, warding off the contagion of evil and removing far from us the tedium of life." [2] Incidentally the word used in this hymn, *taedium,* is a familiar synonym for *acedia.* The whole passage brings out the same contrast between triumphant struggle and sinful inactivity, which was felt in the hymns for the canonical hours. Further citations might be multiplied describing the fortitude and courageous leadership of the martyrs, but two others will suffice. The former serves to indicate the tendency to elaborate the details of martyrdom, in contrast to the simpler treatment of this theme in the more ancient hymns. " For thy sake they trod under foot the madness, violence and savage blows of their persecutors. The hook, roughly tearing their flesh, had no effect upon them nor did it rend their bodies. They are slain with swords like sheep. They make no murmur nor complaint but with silent breast, their spirits, conscious of well-doing, maintain their endurance." [3] By such a method the hymn writer may try to enhance the virtue of fortitude, but the appeal of perfect simplicity is lost. The accounts of martyr heroism, apart from hymns, underwent the same process, as

---

[1] *Ecce pulchra canorum,* S.M., lines 8-12.

[2] *Martyr dei qui unicum,* S.B., stanzas 1, 2.

[3] *Sanctorum meritis inclita gaudia,* S.B., stanzas 3, 4.

popular demand required horrors of detail congenial to its taste.[1]

The final illustration emphasizes once more the position of the martyrs as leaders in spiritual conflict. " Most holy martyrs of the supreme God, most heroic warriors of Christ the king, most powerful leaders of the celestial army, victors in heaven singing to God alleluia." [2] The significance of all this heroic endurance and valiant leadership must be sought not in the details of physical or moral courage on the part of the saints, but in the nature of the strife which cost them their lives. However worthy of emulation the act of sheer fortitude may be, apart from the motive which calls it forth, these men are represented as suffering for a cause. The victory is a victory of the Faith. The motives are manifested as the great ideals of a church militant. The two themes of fortitude and the warfare of the soul are closely interrelated. In the light of martyr hymns the conditions and possibility of victory are made clear. The martyrs, too, were human men and women but they were more than conquerors. Under their leadership the Christian may take courage and march on to victory.

The merits of confessors depend rather upon a career of service and devotion than upon the sacrifice of life. Therefore, they are praised for a variety of high qualities manifested in daily living. It is all summed up in one line thus: " Thou hast followed the footsteps of Christ with devoted faith." [3] Another sequence expresses the thought thus: " Praise him who has secured such great joys, because of the merits in which he abounded, shining like a torch." [4]

[1] For popular details in lives of saints in the Middle Ages, *vide* H. Delehaye, *Legends of the Saints* (London: Longmans, Green & Co., 1907), pp. 77, 88, 91-106.

[2] *Sacratissimi martyres summi dei, Anal. Hymn.*, LI, no. 236, stanza 1.

[3] *Adest nobis dies alma*, S.B., line 6.

[4] *Alma cohors una*, S.M., lines 10, 11.

Specific virtues are often attributed to the confessor. " By
confessing thee continually, O Christ, most holy king, bravely
he trod upon the enemy and his proud train. By the performance of virtues and by faith, by the ordering of his confession, denying the flesh in fasting, he obtains the eternal
feast." [1]   " Holy he was and prudent, humble, modest, sober,
chaste and calm." [2]   Such a recital of virtues must have had
significance in itself, and in another hymn honoring the confessor a definite purpose is revealed. For the first time the
idea of imitating the example of the saint becomes clear.
" Justly counting as loss the transitory pleasures of this
world, rejoicing with the angels of heaven, he gains his rewards. Graciously grant that we may follow in his footsteps. Through his intercession forgive thy servants the
offence of sin." [3]

It is perfectly natural that the cultivation of the virtues by
imitating a great example should be taught in hymns for the
confessors. With the period of persecution far behind it,
the medieval church had only an occasional martyr, chiefly
in the outlying fields of missionary enterprise. The primary
virtue of the martyrs, fortitude, was transferred, in the life
of the Christian, from the physical to the moral plane. But
with the confessor the case was different. There were many
confessors in all periods of Christianity, and especially in the
later Middle Ages when a number of great churchmen were
canonized, among them the group of English saints to which
Osmund (d. 1099) himself belonged. Their virtues could
be imitated in every-day life, and the church was able to
utilize the objective ideal when their praises were celebrated.
It is not claimed, of course, that the teaching of great virtues
is the central interest in the cults of medieval saints, either

[1] *Jesu corona celsior, Anal. Hymn.*, LI, no. 116, stanzas 5, 6.

[2] *Iste confessor domini sacratus*, S.B., lines 5, 6.

[3] *Jesu redemptor omnium*, S.B., stanzas 3, 4.

through hymns or any other device. The saint was venerated chiefly to obtain the benefit of his or her intercessory
power. The supplicant was not saved by practicing the
virtues of the saint but by securing his or her influence in
heaven. Nevertheless, the aspect of imitation of the saintly
example was by no means neglected as the hymn just cited
indicates.

A greater social influence, perhaps, resulted from the
praise of the virgin martyr and the emulation of her merits in
the conventual life. There were eight principal virgin
martyrs, St. Agnes, St. Agatha, St. Cecilia, St. Lucy in the
Roman church, and St. Katherine, St. Barbara, St. Margaret
in the eastern church, who with St. Ursula, were inherited,
so to speak, by medieval Christianity. They became the
leading prototypes of the virgin life. Holy women, not
virgins, were also honored by the church in a sequence
which follows quite closely the praises of the ideal woman of
the Book of Proverbs (chap. 31). The virtues of courage,
purity, prudence and fidelity are attributed to her.[1] It is the
only piece of its kind in the Sarum collection while, on the
other hand, the praises of virgins are multiplied in many
hymns.

In the first place, the virgin shares, equally with the men
who died for their faith, the virtues of courage and fortitude.
" Blessed virgin, bravely enduring all things, nor refusing to
die for a glorious reward, graciously pray for us." [2] Her
courage is in fact, twofold, since the woman must surmount
the weakness of her sex as well as the pains of martyrdom.
" This virgin follower of thine is twice blest, since she subdued the frailty of her flesh and overcame with her flesh the
blood-thirsty world." [3] The virgin martyr is also praised for

[1] *Mulier laudabilis*, S.M., lines 1, 2, 40.
[2] *Exsultemus in hac die festiva*, S.M., verse 17.
[3] *Virginis proles opifexque matris*, S.B., stanza 2.

her abstinence, temperance and her triumphant struggle with sin. " She subdued the flesh by the restraint of fasting and severed herself from lust by the sword of struggle. She fought against all the attacks of the enemy and, relying upon the right hand of Christ, she laid low the blood-stained foe." [1]

In connection with the praise of virgins is used the figure of the ladder of virtues, by which ascent is gained to the ideal life or to the heavenly kingdom. So far, the virtues have been figuratively depicted in very rare instances. One of them, in which the gifts of the wise men symbolize the virtues, has been mentioned in a previous section, and the comparison of certain virtues to the dimensions of Solomon's temple has also been noted. The sequence which contains the figure of the ladder occurs in the Winchester Troper, and is attributed to Notker. The poem celebrates the praises of holy virgins, who, with divine aid, have mounted to heaven by a path so beset with difficulties as to daunt the hardiest spirit. The introduction only is quoted to show the mixture of classical allusions and Christian ideas. Four virtues seem to be emphasized throughout the piece, namely, fortitude, faith, virginity and love, but no regular progression is indicated. Had the thought been more happily expressed, this poem would have deserved a much wider circulation than it actually seems to have secured in medieval England. " A ladder upraised to heaven, girt about with tortures, is continually guarded below by a wary dragon, lest anyone be able, uninjured, to mount to its highest round. An Ethiopian, with drawn sword, threatening death, forbids its ascent. A shining youth, resting upon its top, holds a golden bough. Yet the love of Christ causes this ladder to be so easily ascended by holy women that, treading the dragon underfoot, and passing by the sword of the Ethiopian, through every kind of torments they are able to achieve the summit and

---

[1] *Virginis venerandae de numero*, S.B., lines 4-7.

from the hand of the consoling king receive the golden bough." [1]   The conception of a ladder of virtues was common in the Middle Ages.   Honorius of Autun made use of this idea which was later adapted to pictorial expression and employed in illuminations.[2]

Among the group of hymns which praise the virgin martyrs there is one, *Jesu corona virginum,* which has been prized throughout all the Christian ages.   It has been attributed, with good reason, to Ambrose.   Ambrose explained to his sister Marcellina, in one of his prose works, how the Old Testament had foreshadowed the ideal of life-long virginity and how the New Testament had exalted the Virgin mother of Jesus and confirmed that ideal.[3]   Ambrose reconciled the New to the Old Testament in a symbolic exposition which became the permanent possession of medieval theology. The hymn reflects perfectly his point of view.[4]   " Jesus, crown of virgins, whom that mother conceived and brought forth, uniquely, while a virgin, mercifully receive these vows ; who dost wander among the lilies, encircled with bands of virgins, adorning with glory thy brides, granting them rewards.[5]   Wherever thou dost go the virgins follow and, singing, they accompany thee with praises, sounding sweet hymns." [6]

As the four groups of apostles, martyrs, confessors and virgins have passed in review, a specific virtue has been noted with three of them, namely, justice for the apostles, courage

---

[1] *Scalam ad caelos,* W.T., lines 1-7.

[2] Honorius of Autun, *Speculum Ecclesiae* (PL, clxxii, 869 *et seq.*). E. Mâle, *L'Art religieux du XIIIᵉ Siècle en France* (Paris: Colin, 1902), p. 133 for illustration.

[3] Ambrose, *De Virginibus,* i, 3 (PL, xvi, 191, 194).

[4] Walpole, p. 27.

[5] *Cf. Song of Songs,* 6: 2, 3.

[6] *Jesu corona virginum,* S.B., stanzas 1-3.

for the martyrs and for the virgins chastity, which was regarded as a form of *temperantia*.   The distribution of the
three virtues from the cardinal group in this way, seems to
have become a convention.   John de Burgh, who wrote a
manual for parish priests in England, in the fourteenth
century expressed the idea thus, assigning the fourth virtue,
prudence, to confessors.[1]   " The apostles were an example of
justice for us, the martyrs of fortitude, the confessors of
prudence, the virgins of temperance.—Justice was conspicuous in the apostles, fortitude in the martyrs, prudence in the
confessors and temperance in the virgins." [2]   The generalization is weak in respect to confessors, if references to prudence are sought in the hymns, for one only has assigned this
virtue to them.   A second reference to prudence was found
in connection with the apostles.   Still, the hymns found in
the Common of Saints must be supplemented by those honoring individual confessors before a final evaluation of the
evidence is made.   It happens for instance, that St. Ethelwold, bishop of Winchester and confessor (d. 984), is twice
lauded for his prudence.   " Prudently he disbursed his sacred
talents; " [3] and " Filled with the wisdom of discretion, by
divine grace he enjoyed prudence." [4]

The fact that De Burgh presents current ideas about the
virtues makes it all the more interesting that in one medium

[1] John de Burgh was chancellor of Cambridge University, 1385, and
rector of Collingham. *Vide* J. Bale, *Index Britanniae Scriptorum*, edited
by R. L. Poole (Oxford: Clarendon Press, 1902) ; G. R. Owst, *Preaching in Mediaeval England*, p. 298; F. A. Gasquet, *Parish Life in Mediaeval
England*, p. 220.

[2] *Exemplum iustitiae nobis fuerunt apostoli; fortitudinis martyres;
prudentiae confessores; temperantiae virgines.... Iustitia praeeminebat
in apostolis; fortitudo in martyribus, prudentia in confessoribus, in virginibus temperantia.* Johannes de Burgo, *Pupilla Oculi* (Strassburg:
Johann Schott, 1517), p. clxiiii.

[3] *Laude celebret vox*, W.T., line 15.

[4] *Dies sacra dies ista*, W.T., line 9.

for instruction, the hymn, his generalization is fairly well substantiated. The chief virtues taught in hymns for the Common of Saints are the four great cardinal virtues, justice, fortitude, prudence and temperance. The classification is not so rigid as De Burgh would imply, for apostles, it appears, possess prudence, and virgins display courage, and martyrs are distinguished for temperance. On the other hand, there is an undoubted emphasis which confirms De Burgh's opinion.

As the hymns in the Common of Saints are once more reviewed, the objective human ideal stands forth as the novel feature for ethical teachings. Apostles, martyrs, confessors and virgins are held up for imitation. The characteristics of the approved life are to be inculcated by following in the footsteps of those who have achieved perfection. In the first section of the liturgy this objective method of teaching was used, it is true, in connection with the Divine example of the virtues but the human model of the virtues did not appear. Only in connection with the sins of Herod and Judas was reference made to a human embodiment of specific qualities.

Teaching by objective models rather than by abstractions, tends to awaken a more lively interest in the qualities presented. They are the same characteristics with a new emphasis. Aside from the mention of virtues in general, belonging to all the saints, the actual qualities named are very few and they are narrowed down to the same group which has been found elsewhere. The apostles possess justice but are also praised for prudence and courage. All these virtues are requisite to their functions as judges and as warriors. Martyrs possess courage above all things but are also strong in faith and self-control. The treatment of the martyr theme is clearly developed from its simple and early heroic form to its more elaborate character in hymns of later date. A conventional feature is the persecutor, who after the fashion of Herod, pours out his rage and cruelty upon the victim. The theme of spiritual conflict takes on greater significance in the contribution made by martyr hymns, as the martyrs appear preeminent in leadership. Confessors are distinguished by courage, faith, prudence, humility, and restraint. Virgins possess faith, love, courage and temperance. As martyrs they vie with men in their capacity for suffering. As types of the conventual ideal they are conspicuous for the ascetic virtues.

Hymns for the Common of Saints do not mention specific personages, although it has been noted already that they were employed in the Sarum liturgy for the praise of individual saints. In such cases they resemble in their application, the hymns for the Proper of Saints, to be next considered, in which the objective ideal is more sharply defined.

CHAPTER V

HYMNS FOR THE PROPER OF SAINTS

I. BIBLICAL SAINTS, THE VIRGIN

FROM the point of view of historical development the hymns for the Proper of Saints were the last to be established in the medieval centuries. Up to the twelfth century local calendars were very similar but after the twelfth century a diversification took place as local cults grew up. Moreover, the praises of saints long honored by the church were sung in a multitude of new compositions, especially sequences in the missal. To a great extent, therefore, the poetry to be reviewed in this section reflects the taste and opinion of the period after 1100. Many older compositions appear also. The ideas which are found in the hymns and sequences sung during the thirteenth and fourteenth centuries are either those which had commended themselves for centuries and were now a part of the fabric of Christian thought, or those which expressed current opinion in matters of faith and conduct.

Up to this point the arrangement of material has followed closely the chronology of the liturgical year. With the Proper of Saints, however, a departure from the order of time will be made and the hymns for the various festivals will be discussed as follows: (1) hymns for the feasts which honor Biblical saints, except the Virgin, (2) hymns honoring the Virgin, (3) those for non-Biblical saints, (4) those for later festivals not previously included and especially for All Saints. In concluding this section a brief account of the

system of the seven deadly sins and the seven principal
virtues will be given, as it culminated in the later medieval
period.

Foremost among Biblical saints stand the apostles, including St. Paul. One of the ancient hymns belonging to the
liturgy for the Common of Apostles is *Annue Christe secu-
lorum domine,* which was expanded for the Proper of Saints
by the addition of several stanzas devoted to the individual
apostles. A tendency is observable, even here, to attach a
specific virtue to the saint, or to make him a type of that
virtue. In this way, Matthew and James are singled out as
the possessors of justice.[1] The epithet *just* had been connected with James, the brother of Jesus, from the beginning
and had become traditional. This James, who was the head
of the church in Jerusalem after the death of Jesus, was
identified during the Middle Ages with the apostles of the
same name.[2] Although one of the apostles is meant in the
hymn, the words are: " James the Just, the brother of Jesus,
the Lord." In this same hymn Andrew is praised for meekness.[3] The epithet *mitis,* meaning *gentle* or *meek,* has not
been mentioned before but it occurs some twelve times in
the English collections. It is a quality of the divine nature.[4]
Esther, the Old Testament heroine, is described as meek.[5]
The Virgin is frequently praised for this virtue.[6] St.
Martin possesses it.[7] In fact, meekness is the only virtue

[1] *Annue Christe,* D.H., stanzas 9, 15.

[2] Eusebius, *Hist. Eccle.* ii, 1, 23 (PG, xx, 134, 195). F. Sieffert in
Art. " James ", *New Schaff-Herzog Encyclopedia of Religious Knowledge* (N. Y.: Funk & Wagnalls Co., 1910).

[3] *Annue Christe,* D.H., stanza 7.

[4] *Dulcis Jesus Nazarenus,* S.B., stanza 10a.

[5] *Jubilemus pia mente,* S.M., stanza 11a.

[6] *Ave mundi spes Maria,* S.M., lines 1, 2.

[7] *Martine confessor dei,* D.H., line 16.

praised in hymns, which may be regarded in any way comparable in importance to the seven great virtues. The reason may perhaps be sought in the prominence given to this virtue in the Beatitudes, and in its similarity to humility.[1] Andrew is undoubtedly its chief exponent. This is clear from the hymn already cited and also from the sequence appointed for St. Andrew's feast in the Sarum missal, where he is termed once more "the meekest of the saints."[2] In this poem a brief account of St. Andrew's life is given. He is found preaching in Achaia where he becomes the victim of the persecution under Aegeas, a magistrate of that region.[3] Another sequence, this time from the Winchester Troper, denounces the envy which seems to be the chief motive of the persecutor. "Beholding this, the faithless Aegeas burned overmuch with envy."[4] As the stories of the martyrdom of individual saints proceed, the roll of the historic persecutors will increase in length and the condemnation of their envy, wrath and avarice will grow in intensity.

Peter and Paul are often honored in the same hymns because of the fact that they have a common feast day. They are both judges in the court of heaven. They are the founders of the church. They are united in death at the hand of Nero. "Twin olive trees with a single loyalty, grant that those devoted in faith, strong in hope and filled with the fountain of a twofold love, that greatest of the virtues, may live after the death of the body."[5]

For the first time, the hymns praising the two leading apostles contain mention of the four cardinal virtues in one

[1] *Beati sunt mites quoniam ipsi possidebunt terram* (Matt. 5:4).

[2] *Sacrosancta hodiernae*, S.M., line 3.

[3] For the legend of St. Andrew, *vide Golden Legend* (Temple Classics), II, 99-102.

[4] *Clara cantemus sonoriter*, W.T., line 7.

[5] *Aurea luce et decore roseo*, S.B., stanza 5.

group, possessed by the same individual. " Constant in courage, justice, temperance and prudence." [1] This is a most interesting passage because it illustrates the use of *virtus* in the classic sense as a synonym for *fortitudo*. The fact of three other specific qualities being combined closely with *virtus* proves its significance. In another early poem honoring the same saints the cardinal virtues are associated with St. Paul. " Then Paul directs the way to noble living; he preaches justice, consecrates prudence, presses on with the greatest courage, and is temperate in all things." [2] Both St. Peter and St. Paul are conspicuous for faith. " The faith of Christ crowned those who followed God as their leader. The first was Peter the Apostle nor was Paul inferior in grace. The chosen vessel of the Lord equaled the faith of Peter." [3] Although faith is a characteristic of both, Peter is more frequently lauded for this particular virtue because his faith is the foundation of the church. " A glorious light is present glowing at the festival of the Apostle, when the church, built upon the faith of Peter, celebrates his praises." [4] Again, " The church has its foundation in the faith of Peter and its bulwark in the dogma of Paul." [5] Peter stands as a type of faith, just as Andrew is the type of meekness.

Paul, before his conversion, had been a persecutor of the earliest church, and had been guilty of the sins of pride and anger. " Moved by fury, he breathed out dread violence,

[1]   Constans virtute et iustitia, temperantia et prudentia.
    Laude jocunda melos turma, S.M., lines 15, 16.

[2] *Sanctus Petrus et magnus Paulus*, W.T., stanza 8b. This sequence has a counterpart in the Limoges collection. The Limoges version is used above as the probable original form. *Vide Anal. Hymn.*, VII, no. 181.

[3] *Apostolorum passio, Anal. Hymn.*, L. no. 15, lines 7-12.

[4] *Sollemnitate rutilans apostolica*, W.T., lines 1-3.

[5] *In solemni memoria*, Y.M., verse 11.

and with the most cruel slaughter he savagely tortured the members of Christ. Lo, a light from heaven shining about him, deprives him of sight but confers upon him spiritual vision. It buffets him, lest his pride continue; it lays him low but raises him up from falling; it rebukes him when prostrate but, in rebuking, heals him." [1] Paul was destined himself, to perish by the act of the persecutor, and with him St. Peter. "They achieved heaven", says one poet, "through the fury of Nero." [2] Again, "Nero, raving in madness kindles the torches more and more. He commands Peter to be crucified and Paul to be slain with the dreadful sword." [3] Finally as martyrs, they became victors in spiritual warfare, able to defend their weaker fellows, hard pressed on earth. "Therefore, ye glorious martyrs, blessed Peter, and Paul lily of the world, triumphant warriors of the heavenly court, by your gracious prayers defend us from all evils and bear us up on high." [4]

The tendency to depict individual saints as types of special virtues, already noticed in two instances, St. Andrew and St. Peter, is much more strongly felt in the praises of St. John the Baptist, St. John the Evangelist and St. Stephen. Here, the group of Biblical saints must be enlarged to include, not only apostles, but others prominent in the early pages of Christian history.

St. John the Baptist is preeminently the type of the ascetic ideal. His life in the wilderness gains significance in that it constitutes an example for the hermit life of the earlier ascetic practice and of individuals throughout the medieval centuries. The Sarum breviary contains a lengthy hymn of thirteen stanzas recounting the details of his life. The

[1] *Sollempnitas sancti Pauli*, S.M., lines 6-12.
[2] *Sanctus Petrus, magnus Paulus*, W.T., line 16.
[3] *Hac in die recolatur*, Y.M., stanza 7.
[4] *Felix per omnes festum*, Y.B., stanza 8.

hymn is divided into three shorter hymns for the services of
the feast.   Three stanzas describing his hermit life run as
follows: " A youth of tender age, thou didst seek the caves
of the desert, fleeing from the throngs of thy fellows, so as
to keep thy life from stain by foolish speech.   The camel
gave thee a shaggy covering and a sheepskin was bound about
thy sacred loins.   Thy drink was water and thy food wild
honey and locusts.—O thou greatly blest and worthy of the
highest merit, thy purity all unspotted, especially powerful
martyr and hermit, greatest of the prophets." [1]   The circumstances leading up to John's execution offered an opportunity to exalt the ideal of truth.   This is one of the very
few instances in which the virtue of truth is lauded.   " He is
imprisoned, to whom truth is precious.—For the love of
truth thou dost shine in the honor of a blessed martyrdom." [2]

St. John the Evangelist is regarded chiefly as the type of
purity, although his faith and love are also worthy of emulation.   The quality of faith is ascribed to St. John in a very
interesting hymn which has been handed down from the
early centuries and may have been written by Ambrose.[3]
The Sea of Galilee where St. John once followed a fisher's
vocation, becomes in the vision of the poet, the sea of life
whose waves, through faith, the disciple rides with safety.
Swiftly changing his metaphor, the poet now sees the fisher-
man drawing from the waters the fish which is the Word of
God, or in a succeeding stanza, the faith thereby inspired.[4]
It is quite impossible to determine whether the author of this

---

[1] *Antra deserti teneris sub annis*, S.B., stanzas 1, 2.   *O nimis felix
meritique celsi*, S.B., stanza 1.   For a briefer version, *vide Deo laudes
gloriose concinat*, Y.M., lines 8-10.

[2] *Deo laudes gloriose concinat.*, Y.M., lines 15, 24.

[3] *Amore Christi nobilis, Anal. Hymn.*, L, no. 9.   For the authorship *vide*
Walpole, p. 57.

[4] *Amore Christi nobilis*, stanzas 2-4.

hymn had in mind the symbolism of the sacred fish, but it is highly probable. In the year 200 the idea of the Logos-Ichthys was already current in Alexandria. This symbolism appeared in connection with baptism as the baptismal water when consecrated, was thought to bear Christ, the fish, referred to as the Logos.[1]

Love is also figuratively ascribed to St. John. " But John, the eagle of love with twin wings is borne in the pattern of the divine, in purer light." [2] To identify him with the eagle of Ezekiel's vision is a commonplace of Christian art and literature (Ezek. 1 : 10). The novel feature is the association of love with the symbolism of the eagle, which is ordinarily conceived as a type of aspiration to divine heights.

Two sequences exalt the act of the Evangelist in renouncing earthly ties for heavenly love, one from the liturgy of Sarum, the other from that of York. " O John, virgin disciple whom Jesus loved, thou didst leave for love of him thy earthly father in the ship. Thou didst forego wedlock to follow the Messiah. — Triumphant upon the cross, Christ gave thee to be the guardian of his mother, that, thyself a virgin, thou mightest cherish the Virgin and care for her." [3] " Summoned, he left his father, the ship and the nets, following first the voice of the Redeemer, and then his footsteps ; O what great trust !—When the king was suffering the penalty of death upon the cross, a virgin received a Virgin to be cared for in ward. O what great chastity ! " [4]

John's persecution and exile are treated in the familiar way. There is praise for his courage in the face of hard-

---

[1] F. J. Dölger, ΙΧΘΥΣ (Munter: Aschendorffschen Buchdruckerei, 1928), I, pp. 17-18, 68-69.

[2] *Jocundare plebs fidelis*, Y.M., stanza 10.

[3] *Johannes, Jesu Christo multum dilecte virgo*, S.M., lines 1-4, 8, 9.

[4] *Virgo mater gratuletur*, Y.M., stanzas 3, 5.

ships inflicted by the wrath of his tormentor, this time the emperor Domitian.[1]

The last of the Biblical saints to be singled out as types of one special virtue is St. Stephen, who surpassed the others in displaying a love sufficiently unselfish to include his enemies. " O love eternal, all the saints through the ages possess thee, among whom Stephen, the deacon and protomartyr is resplendent in his crown of glory." [2] " O Stephen, saint and protomartyr precious in the sight of God, who wast wholly surrounded by the virtue of love, thou didst pray to God for thine enemies. Pour out thy prayers now for us who honor thee, that the Master, propitiated by thy intercession may unite us, cleansed us from sins, with the citizens of heaven." [3] The circumstances of Stephen's martyrdom and his unselfish fortitude, perennially appealing, could not fail to attract the medieval hymn writers.[4]

Passing to the women saints of the Biblical narrative, those who receive the highest praises in hymns are St. Mary Magdalene and St. Mary the Virgin. The Virgin hymns are so numerous and important that they will be discussed separately in a later section. An incidental reference should here be made to St. Anne, the mother of the Virgin, whose great importance would seem to demand recognition in hymns. Such hymns belong to the feast of St. Anne but they represent the saint in a light reflected from the glories of her daughter. Humility is the chief of her virtues: " Mother holy and humble of whom Mary was born." [5]

With the exception of the Virgin and possibly St. Anne, St. Mary Magdalene has enjoyed the greatest popularity and

[1] *Virgo mater gratuletur*, Y.M., stanza 8.

[2] *Conserva super hanc familiam*, Y.B., lines 8-12.

[3] *Sancte dei preciose prothomartyr Stephane*, S.B., stanzas 1, 2.

[4] *Magnus deus in universa terra*, S.M., lines 18-21.

[5] *In Annae puerperio*, S.B., line 9.

influence of all the women saints of the Bible. She is the unquestioned prototype of the penitent woman just as the dying
thief is regarded as the supreme example of the penitent man.
It was only to be expected that the sins most abhorrent to the
medieval Christian should be fastened upon her, to heighten
the effect of her contrition. One of her hymns illustrates
quite remarkably the ideas of the age. " Praise, O mother
church, praise the mercy of Christ, who washes away the
seven sins through the grace of the sevenfold Spirit. Mary,
the sister of Lazarus, who committed so many sins, returns
from the jaws of hell itself to the threshold of eternal life." [1]
Here the seven sins appear to be the demons cast out of the
spirit of the Magdalene by Jesus. Grace is imparted through
the seven gifts. There is a possibility that the symbolism
suggested by the mention of seven demons in the Biblical
narrative (Mark 16: 9, Luke 8:2) may have had something
to do with fixing the number of the deadly sins at seven,
especially in view of the corresponding concept of seven gifts
of the Holy Spirit. Another reference in a hymn likewise
in honor of St. Mary Magdalene partially confirms the same
supposition. " Thou dost cleanse her of seven demons by
the seven-fold Spirit." [2] Greater weight is given to the
theory by a passage from the writings of Gregory the Great,
who was the first of the influential supporters of the number
seven rather than eight. In one of his homilies on the
Gospels, he mentions the story of St. Mary Magdalene, explaining that the seven demons are symbolic of sins.[3] Incidentally, Gregory, like the author of the first hymn quoted,
identifies Mary Magdalene with Mary, the sister of Lazarus.

Prayer, as well as sermon and hymn, points to the same

[1] *Lauda mater ecclesia*, Y.B., stanzas 1, 2.

[2] *Laus tibi, Christe*, Y.M., verse 16.

[3] Gregory the Great, *Homiliae in evangelia*, ii (PL, lxxvi, 1239). *Et quid per septem daemonia nisi universa vitia designatur?*

figurative meaning attached to the seven demons of the narrative. A petition in the Sarum missal, to be used before the observance of the canonical hours, presents the fully rounded symbolism of the number seven in the most intricate detail. The clause which is of particular interest here runs as follows: " May I in such wise please Thee, that, through the painful exercise of the mystic septenary in the practise of the seven works of the spirit, I may be enabled to avoid the seven deadly sins, which are the seven devils cast out of that Mary of the Gospels by Christ." [1]   When one considers the extraordinary prominence of St. Mary Magdalene in all ages of Christian belief, it is easier to understand the importance of these hymns as a witness to the concept of seven sins.

Humility, a condition of penitence, logically characterizes St. Mary Magdalene whose prayers are potent above. " O mother holy and humble, mindful of our frail nature, do thou pilot us by thy prayers through the waters of this life." [2] With her humility, the author of another hymn contrasts the pride of the Pharisee at whose home she anointed the feet of Jesus. Mary is the figure of the church and, in the contemptuous attitude of the Pharisee, is seen the pride which expresses itself in heretical attack. " By this proselyte, O Christ, thou dost signify the church whom thou dost summon, an alien, to the table of thy sons. Amidst the feast of the law and the marks of grace, the pride of the Pharisee attacks her with leprous heresy." [3] The association of the sins of heresy and pride is strictly in accordance with medieval teaching, as has been noticeable in the analysis of pride already given from the writings of Regino.

Before leaving the group of Biblical saints, the praises of

[1] A. H. Pearson, *Sarum Missal*, translated (London: Church Printing Co., 1884), p. 270.

[2] *Aeterni patris unice*, Y.B., stanza 6.

[3] *Laus tibi Christe*, Y.M., verses 18, 19.

the archangels, Michael, Raphael and Gabriel call for more than passing notice. Foremost in the angelic hierarchies, they are depicted as the supreme leaders in spiritual warfare, outranking all lesser chieftains of the church militant. "All ye holy seraphim and cherubim, thrones and dominations, principalities, powers, virtues, angels and archangels, praise and honor is due unto you. Ye ninefold ranks of blessed spirits whom love has strengthened in the praises of God, strengthen us frail mortals by your prayers. Valiantly conquering by your aid our weaknesses of the spirit, now and forever may we be worthy to share in your holy solemnities." [1]

Each of the archangels is separately exalted in hymns as a leader of the heavenly armies. "Let Gabriel, brave angel, fly from above to repel the ancient enemy." [2] Reference is made to Raphael in the following: "What word can tell, what writing describe, the powers possessed by the holy angels that they may be able to protect their knights and direct them to heaven by the appointed path." [3] Michael outranks Gabriel and Raphael. "Let us reverently praise all the warriors of heaven but especially the commander-in-chief of the celestial army, Michael, who in his might crushes under foot the Prince of Darkness." [4] As patron saint of the church militant and commander-in-chief of the heavenly army St. Michael has no peer in the warfare of the soul. As victor over the enemies of God's people and the hosts of hell, trampling upon the dragon, St. Michael is resplendent with the associations both of Hebrew tradition and Christian symbolism. [5] He is the leader, vivid and terrible, exalted in

[1] *Omnes sancti seraphim,* W.T., lines 1-9.

[2] *Christe sanctorum decus angelorum,* S.B., lines 9, 10.

[3] *Excelsorum civium inclita gaudia,* H.B., stanza 4.

[4] *Tibi Christe, splendor patris,* S.B., lines 4-6.

[5] For a summary of Michael's place in Hebrew tradition, *vide Jewish Encyclopedia.*

the thought of the Middle Ages as the unknown author of
this hymn has exalted him.   He is represented similarly
countless times in literature and art.[1]   England boasts 721
dedications in honor of St. Michael or St. Michael and All
Angels, most of them dating from the medieval period.   No
wonder that the sculptured representations of spiritual combat in medieval England were more apt to reflect this particular inspiration, and the hymns as well.[2]

The attitude of the worshipper has been clearly revealed in
the praises of the archangels, his weakness and dependence
upon the strength of celestial leadership.   Perhaps the greatest of all such prayers for assistance in the struggle against
sin, is that of St. Gildas, from whose *Lorica* the following
stanzas have been selected for translation.   "And I beseech likewise the supernal virtues of the heavenly host that
they do not abandon me to be torn by my enemies, but defend
me now with their mighty weapons.   And may they lead me
in the battle of the celestial army, cherubim, seraphim,
Michael and Gabriel with a multitude of others.   I pray the
thrones, virtues, archangels, principalities, powers and angels
to defend me in the thick of the fight, that I may be able to
lay low mine enemies.   Moreover, I beseech those other um-
pires, patriarchs, prophets four times four, apostles, pilots
of the ship of Christ, and the martyrs and all the athletes of
the church, that through their aid, safety may gird me about
and all evil perish from me; that Christ may make alliance
with me and that fear and trembling may take possession of
the hateful ranks of my foes."[3]

[1] Typical treatments may be found in *Golden Legend* (Temple Classics),
V, 188; P. H. Ditchfield, *Cathedrals of Gt. Britain* (London: Dent, 1916),
p. 238, sculptured figure in Lichfield cathedral.

[2] F. Arnold-Forster, *Studies in Church Dedications* (London: Skeffington, 1899), I, p. 37; F. Bond, *Dedications and Patron Saints of
English Churches* (London: Milford, Oxford Univ. Press, 1914), p. 17.

[3] *Suffragare trinitas unitas, Anal. Hymn.,* LI, no. 262, stanzas 3-7.

With the praises of the archangels the theme of spiritual warfare reaches its climax in medieval hymns. The hardy virtues of the Stoic ideal were the first weapons which the earliest hymns commended in the struggle with sin. The idea of opposed or contrasted virtues and sins has been found, in accordance with the allegorical method which Prudentius made familiar in his *Psychomachia* and *Hamartigenia* already mentioned in a previous chapter. The martyrs, as victorious champions of the faith have been portrayed in the role of leaders. Chivalry and knighthood have been influential in re-affirming and interpreting the Pauline ideal of the spiritual warrior side by side with the monastic pattern of the approved life. Both are merged in hymns as the knight and monk are merged in the crusading orders. It will presently be observed that many a saint is termed *miles Christi* in hymns. A question at once arises as to the association of ideas established in the minds of medieval people by these words. In medieval Latin the word *miles* meant *knight*,[1] and there can be no reasonable doubt that such was the familiar connotation of the term. Were other evidence lacking, art would supply the testimony, for the saints acquired the armor of contemporary warfare in artistic representation.[2] From the point of view of the moral qualifications for knighthood which are found in codes of chivalry, a strong resemblance is apparent between them and the list of virtues which are prominent in hymns.[3] Secular literature offers its testimony that the struggle with sin is alle-

[1] *Vide* Du Cange.

[2] A. M. Jameson, *Sacred and Legendary Art* (London: Longmans Green & Co., 1866), I, p. 100 (St. Michael).

[3] W. C. Meller, *A Knight's Life in the Days of Chivalry* (London: Laurie, 1924), Moral qualifications for knighthood, pp. 49-60. From the *Code of Chivalry* Meller quotes as follows: "Coutumes exigées d'un Chevalier, savoir sept vertus, dont trois théologales, foy, espérance et charité: et quatre cardinales—justice, prudence, force et attempérance."

gorically portrayed in terms of knighthood, for the story of Galahad's combat with seven knights representing the seven deadly sins, is well-known.   It has been depicted in art by Sir Edwin Abbey who made this scene an integral part of his frieze of the Holy Grail.[1]

Such considerations greatly strengthen the position taken in this section that medieval hymns picture the saint, not only as a leader in spiritual warfare but as a knightly champion; that the ideal Christian battles with the hosts of evil under the banner of the saint, carrying upon his lips the very names of those to whom he was accustomed to appeal in the war cries of feudal strife.

The north portal of the Cathedral of Laon was consecrated to the Virgin.   Here may be seen the sculptured decoration depicting the triumphant virtues towering over the conquered vices.   The artist is at one with the theologian in the logic of his design, for both point to the Virgin as the possessor of every virtue.[2]   The qualities which are personified by the sculptor in this decoration, which belongs to the last part of the twelfth century, are sobriety, chastity, patience, love, faith, humility, gentleness, and liberality.[3]   It is a typical list, containing some of the principal virtues but not restricted to them.   The hymns, likewise, which honor the Virgin, reveal in the same variety the virtues which adorn her character.

Quite apart from the belief in the complete sinlessness of the Virgin, it was commonly held that every virtue flowered in her character.   The discussion of the doctrine of the Immaculate Conception and the observance of its related festival from the twelfth century did not take place without heated

[1] Malory, *Mort d'Arthur*, Book XIII, chaps. 15-16.   The Holy Grail frieze is in the Boston Public Library.

[2] L. Broche, *La Cathédrale de Laon* (Paris: Laurens, 1926), pp. 65, 66.

[3] *Sobrietas, castitas, patientia, caritas, fides, humilitas, mansuetudo* and *largitas.   Vide* E. Mâle, *L'Art religieux du XIIIe Siècle en France* (Paris: Colin, 1902), pp. 130, 179.

controversy upon this point. The solution of the difficulty
proved a simple one, at least that solution which is preserved
in the correspondence between Nicholas, prior of St. Albans
and Peter of Celles, afterwards bishop of Chartres. Peter
contended that the Virgin may have been subject to temptation, at least before the birth of Jesus. Nicholas maintained
that she had not experienced temptation. The significance
of all this in a study of ethical and religious ideals is clear.
Virtue must be achieved, not miraculously conferred, if it
is to be the inspiration of other human lives. After extended debate Nicholas arrived at a conclusion which may
be paraphrased thus: Mary's virtuous qualities and actions
did not result from a struggle with manifold temptations.
That she was tempted to commit the grosser sins, at any
rate, was unthinkable. Her virtues were the response to
the external material conditions of life in which she found
herself, and the result of her contemplation of the divine.[1]
This point of view, which evidently proved satisfactory to
Peter of Celles, will be found very helpful in considering the
virtues of Mary as they appear in hymns.

Beginning with the hymns which recite the general praises
of the Virgin, apart from a particular episode in her life, a
variety of virtues are found to be prominent. She is called
holy, exalted, benign, delightful, merciful, compassionate
and *meek*.[2] There is considerable emphasis placed upon

[1] J. E. Bridgett, *Our Lady's Dowry* (London: Burns & Oates, no date),
4th edition, pp. 25-30. Peter of Celles, *Epistula* clxxii (PL, ccii, 625).
More quippe nostro esurivit, sitivit, friguit, et multis tribulationibus de-
cocta, nostris calamitatibus subjacuit, et ex talium in Christo patientia,
multimoda meritorum praerogativa efflorint, absque his quibus intrinsecus
quotidie proficiebat: nova videlicet virginitatis dilectione, singulari dei
contemplatione, incompatibili proximi charitate, tota virtutum omnium pul-
chritudine, nulla maculae vel levissimae turpitudine.

[2] *Ave mundi spes Maria*, S.M., verse 13; *Virgini Mariae laudes intonant*,
Y.M., line 8; *Ave Maria gratia plena*, S.M., line 12; *Stabat juxta Christi*
crucem, Y.M., line 30.

meekness, a virtue mentioned elsewhere as attributed to Mary. Its close relation to humility is thus made clear: " Take away pride, thou our infinite safety, take the proud and make them meek and pure." [1]   Thus the virtue of Mary may be conferred upon the worshipper.   A lengthy sequence from the York missal contains a remarkable list of Mary's virtues, among them mercy, love, modesty, purity, long-suffering, equity.[2]   All the virtues are hers in many figurative concepts: among them, " Let now the holy lyre re-echo, sounding to God the fair theme of her virtues.   This is the harmony of the virtues flowing with its divine music." [3]

It is difficult, even if profitable, to thread one's way through the maze of medieval theology upon the subject of the Virgin, to the inner court where stands the simple and gracious figure of Mary, the Hebrew maiden.   Whatever survives of this purely human approach seems to be perpetuated in the liturgy for the feasts of the Presentation of the Blessed Virgin, and of the Visitation.   From this angle, the virtues of Mary possess a universal attraction.   The story of Mary's birth, her life in the Temple, and her espousal to Joseph, are told in the apocryphal *Gospel of the Nativity of Mary* and *Gospel of Pseudo-Matthew,* which are also the source of the hymns relating to these matters.   As the former Gospel was incorporated very largely in the *Golden Legend,* this material became a part of popular belief, well-known to the Middle Ages in literature and in art.[4]

[1] *Salve sancta parens,* S.M., stanza 5.

[2] *Ave gloriosa virginum regina,* Y.M., lines 5, 18, 21, 22, 28, 54.

[3] *Claris vocibus inclyta,* W.T., lines 4, 5.

[4] For the English text *vide Ante-Nicene Fathers,* American Reprint (Buffalo: Christian Lit. Co., 1886), vol. viii; M. R. James, *Apocryphal New Testament* (Oxford: Clarendon Press, 1924), Analyses, pp. 73, 79, 80; *Golden Legend* (Temple Classics), V, pp. 99-103. For the Latin liturgical text *vide Sarum Breviary,* II, 345-349. With slight omissions this is the same as *Pseudo-Matthew,* chaps. 1-6 inc.

The period of Mary's sojourn in the temple is marked by the manifestation of many specific virtues as well as all virtue. " So much did the virtue and grace of her tender childhood increase, as she fulfilled in every act the commands of the creator. She is obedient to the familiar voice of the Holy Spirit. The adornment of every virtue of the inner life shines forth from the character of the Virgin." [1] " Instructed, perfected, strong in character and admirable in repute, climbing the steep places by virtue, she is accessible to all, and humble." [2] " By the will of the Eternal Father, she is established in the temple as a virgin, where she enjoys rare delights in contemplation. Devoted to prayer and to the divine duties, utterly hidden from the world, she applies herself to secret studies. Oh strange bounties of the grace bestowed upon the Virgin, which are all fragrance and pleasing to the power on high. Mind, tongue, flesh, spirit, sense, disposition, action, reveal that she has been chosen of heaven to be the mother of the Son of God." [3]

The episode of the Visitation of the Virgin to Elizabeth has also inspired its appropriate hymns, which are apt to share the mood of tender affection which surrounds this scene. Even in a hymn like *Mundi salus affutura,* although overladen with the familiar typology belonging to the Virgin theme, the simpler phrases appear. " The future blessing of the world, far-famed Virgin mother, simple in act, pure in mind, and shining in beauty,—Virgin dear to all hearts, ardent in the desire of love." [4] More pleasing compositions describe the Visitation thus: " The flower of the virtues proceeds from the holy tabernacle. The fragrance of Mary pervades the winding path of the mountain. Out of her

[1] *Sacrae parentis virginis,* S.B., stanzas 3, 4.
[2] *Omnes fideles plaudite,* S.B., stanza 3.
[3] *Aeterni patris ordine,* S.B., stanzas 1-4.
[4] *Mundi salus affutura,* S.B., lines 1-4, 25, 26.

budding love she comes to Elizabeth and in the height of holiness, devoutly she visits her.—Grant, most holy Virgin, adequate aid; since thou art the most generous of mothers, visit us upon earth." [1] " Now is the theme of the feast the grace of abounding love.—Let all the earth be glad, let the whole heart celebrate the sweet Visitation feast, the kindness of a sympathetic heart, the great humility of the Virgin's act, and its sacred solace." [2] The theme of the Visitation to Elizabeth often suggests a spiritual visitation to the hearts of men, bringing with it benefits of grace and love. [3] In one instance the gifts of the Holy Spirit are thus conveyed. " Come, send with greater favor, the gifts of the Holy Spirit that we may be directed to more virtuous paths in the acts of this life." [4] A hymn which commemorates several of the events of Mary's life praises her for her humility when she presents Jesus in the temple, thus emphasizing a virtue which is primarily characteristic of the Visitation scene. [5] We know from other sources how consistent with medieval thought was this idea. A homily of Bede upon the Visitation theme praises the humility of the Virgin in these terms: " Since the human race had perished by the contagion of the pestilence of pride it was fitting that, at the very first outset of the time of salvation, some manifestation should take place of the humility by which we are healed.—And not to angels only but to men does she show humility, and such is her height of virtue, she humbles herself even to her inferiors." [6]

Annunciation hymns are full of Mary's praises. She exhibits faith and meekness in the reception of Gabriel's mes-

[1] *De sacro tabernaculo*, H.B., stanzas 1, 2, 7.

[2] *Celebremus in hac die*, S.M., stanzas 2a, 3.

[3] *De sacro tabernaculo*, H.B., line 28.

[4] *Veni praecelsa domina*, Y.M., stanza 7.

[5] *Mittit ad sterilem*, S.M., stanza 8.

[6] Quoted by J. E. Bridgett, *Our Lady's Dowry*, p. 76.

sage. Her prudence and humility have merited recognition both human and divine.[1] Her faith is once more recalled in a sequence for the Assumption.[2]

Of the virtues which have become familiar in liturgical hymns, *castitas,* with its related adjective *casta* are used over and over again as practically synonymous with the name of the Virgin. It must be understood that these words when applied to the Virgin, stand quite outside the scope of the present study, since the doctrine of the Virgin Birth places the whole matter beyond the limit of the moral category which is under consideration.

Summing up the evidence of the hymns to the Virgin in the words of one of them, " Incomparable in all the universe, never was there one like unto thee," [3] Mary occupies a unique position as an exemplar of all the virtues, especially faith, love and purity. In the cardinal group even justice in the sense of equity (*equitas*) is said to be hers, although this quality is not elsewhere in these hymns predicated of women. In the theological group, hope is the only quality which is not clearly defined in hymns to the Virgin. The word *spes* is used in the sense of the hymn, " Hail, Mary, hope of the world." [4] No doubt there was little thought for any other meaning when the supreme importance of Mary's place in the plan of salvation occupied the minds of people of every degree of culture. On the other hand, certain of the principal virtues are made more significant, since many qualities possessed by the Virgin illustrate, for example, the finer shades of meaning which may be included in a concept such as love.

[1] *Aureo ore primae matris Evae,* W.T., line 9; *Ave maris stella,* S.B., stanza 5; *Proloquium altum recitemus,* S.M., stanzas 3, 5, lines 1, 2.

[2] *Ave praeclara maris stella,* S.M., line 4.

[3] *Proloquium altum recitemus,* S.M., stanza 3.

[4] *Ave, mundi spes Maria,* S.M.

Tracing the theme of Mary's virtues apart from the testimony of hymns the same interesting variety is observable. It was a favorite subject of Ambrose both in his poetical works and in his prose writings. In the *De Virginibus* he devotes a chapter to the virtues of the Virgin, in the course of which he refers to Mary's chastity, goodness, humility, seriousness, prudence, reticence, studiousness and moderation in eating. He says, " Thus she fulfilled all the obligations of virtue." Toward the close of his exposition he asks, " What great virtues are conspicuous in one virgin? The secret of modesty, the banner of faith, the obedience of devotion." [1] These praises are reflected in the hymn *Intende, qui regis Israel* which sometimes opens with the second stanza *Veni, redemptor gentium*.[2] The most significant line in this connection is *Vexilla virtutum micant* (line 11) which preserves the characteristic phraseology of its author and at the same time gives freedom to the devoted worshipper to interpret the words as the loyal enthusiasm of his heart may suggest. The hymn contains mention of one specific quality only, modesty, to which reference has already been made.

Throughout the medieval centuries may be traced the development of the idea which Ambrose expressed. A well-known poem by Peter Damian (d. 1072) illustrates its form in verse. " Grace has made thee gracious to all, has clothed thee with the lily and adorned thee with the rose, has made thee fair with the flowers of the virtues, and altogether radiant." [3] Adam of St. Victor is, above all medieval writers, the poet of the Virgin. " Thou bearest the matchless palm; thou hast no peer on earth nor in the court of heaven. Lauded by all mankind, thou dost possess beyond others the

---

[1] Ambrose, *De Virginibus*, ii, 2 (PL, xvi, 208 *et seq.*).

[2] Walpole, *Early Latin Hymns*, pp. 50-51.

[3] *Rhythmus super salutatione angelica*, stanza 3 (PL, cxlv, 940).

distinction of the virtues." [1]   The prayers of Anselm of Canterbury contain phrases which set apart the Virgin as the source of all virtue. " Therefore without thee there is no piety, no goodness, because thou art the mother of virtue and of all the virtues." [2]   Honorius of Autun, who, like so many of the theologians, found his inspiration to exalt the Virgin in the Song of Songs, attributes to her every virtue but says in one place that she possesses the cardinal virtues. Commenting upon the phrase *Lectus* (or *lectulus*) *noster floridus,* (Cant. 1 : 15) he says: " Flowering, that is, in virtues; she was moreover the house of God, in which he dwelt. The timbers of this house are the chief virtues, prudence, courage, justice, temperance." [3]

Bernard of Clairvaux expressly points to the four great virtues in a similar connection. For his sermon upon the text " Wisdom hath builded her house" (Prov. 9: 1) he interprets the house as the Virgin and its seven columns as follows: Three of the columns represent faith in accordance with the three persons of the Trinity. Four of the columns represent morals in accordance with the four cardinal virtues. [4]

Albertus Magnus treats the subject of Mary's virtues at considerable length. In a series of twelve books, *De Laudibus Mariae Virginis,* he devotes one to the theme of the seven great virtues as displayed in Mary's character, giving the greater space to her faith, hope and love." [5]

[1] *Salve mater salvatoris,* stanza 8. *Vide* E. Misset et P. Aubry, *Les Proses d'Adam de Saint-Victor* (Paris: Welter, 1900).

[2] *Ergo sine te nihil pietatis est, nihilque bonitatis, quia mater virtutis et virtutum es omnium.* (PL, cxlviii, 945).

[3] *Floridus, scilicet in virtutibus. Ipsa etiam domus Dei, in qua habitavit. Ligna principales ejus virtutes, prudentia, fortitudo, justitia, temperantia. Sigillum Beatae Mariae* (PL, clxxii, 502).

[4] PL, clxxxiii, 675, 676.

[5] Albertus Magnus, *Opera Omnia* (Paris: Vivès, 1898), xxxvi, p. 15 *et seq.*

The saints as exemplars of the virtues have been conceived in the light of moral guides whose lives and acts are fit objects of men's emulation.   It is reasonable to suppose that they played a genuine and unmistakable role in the uplift of humanity.   The definite group of virtues which are known as the seven principal virtues possesses in itself an intrinsic value for social and moral progress.   Granting that this is valid, what shall be said of the influence of the cult of the Virgin in exalting these same virtues in everyday life?

To some minds the mass of legend and romance which surrounds the Virgin cult in the Middle Ages makes a travesty of religion.   To other minds it affords a precious revelation of the thoughts of people who looked to her for protection and mercy.   Behind the trivial, the exaggerated, or perhaps the sacrilegious details which are to be found in this literature, there stands the love of Mary.   Sometimes her devotees have but the one redeeming quality, their veneration for her, without which their hope of salvation would have been utterly lost.   In itself, this constitutes a potential social influence.[1]   Henry Adams sees in the Virgin the social ideal of the twelfth and thirteenth centuries, and in the creation of the French Gothic cathedral a monument to her cult which, in a peculiar way, illustrates its far-reaching influence in contemporary society,[2] although this author is not thinking altogether of the cultivation of ideal qualities in the individuals who constructed or thronged the great cathedral shrines.   Approaching the Virgin cult from another direction entirely, what shall be said of possible moral benefit derived from fasts, alms-giving, masses, feasts, pilgrimages

---

[1] For a full discussion of the sources for the tales of the Virgin, *vide* G. G. Coulton, *Five Centuries of Religion* (Cambridge: Univ. Press, 1923), vol. i, appendix 19, *Mary Legends*.

[2] H. Adams, *Mont-Saint-Michel and Chartres*, especially chapters VI, XI, XIII.

and other devotional acts in honor of Mary?[1]   Still another
aspect of the problem has been considered by Father Jarrett,
who sees in the devotion to the Virgin a powerful social influence counteracting the forces of a deteriorating chivalry
in the later Middle Ages.   " The devotion of the Cistercians
and of the North to ' Our Lady ' placed her at the apex of
the chivalry of the twelfth and thirteenth centuries, and perhaps alone prevented the passionate and sentimental roman-
ticism of the fourteenth and fifteenth centuries from growing worse than it did.   It is difficult not to exaggerate the
importance of this devotion in the midst of the boisterous
and rude awakening to beauty which the eleventh and twelfth
centuries developed and made sensitive.   It is only necessary
to look at the art of the whole of our period to see now what
might so easily have been a terribly destructive force became
sublimated into a power for good." [2]

Whatever may be argued from medieval art or from
medieval literature apart from hymnology, respecting the
influence of the cult of the Virgin, one thing seems clear from
the hymns of the English collections,—the Virgin is the
embodiment of every virtue and the supreme object of
emulation among the ranks of the saints.

[1] This aspect of the Virgin cult has been treated by Bridgett, *Our
Lady's Dowry*, pp. 155-351 *passim*.

[2] B. Jarrett, *Social Theories of the Middle Ages* (London: Benn,
1926), p. 92.

CHAPTER VI

Hymns for the Proper of Saints

II. SAINTS NOT MENTIONED IN THE BIBLE; FEASTS OF TRANSFIGURATION, NAME OF JESUS, ALL SAINTS

In order to perceive more clearly the extent to which the saints in this group exhibit the virtues which were characteristic of the approved life, the citations will be grouped with reference to the qualities which are praised. Attention will thus be centered upon the virtues rather than upon their possessors. In a few cases where the personality of the saint is too impressive to be overlooked, the hymns honoring that individual will be examined more closely.

It must be obvious by this time that hymns for saints describe them as the possessors of all the virtues. Such phrases as " shining with the grace of the virtues," " a vessel of the virtues," " through the merits of his virtues ", " in all the glory of the virtues ", " remarkable in virtues ", are common enough.[1] A juxtaposition of the words for virtues and sins often emphasizes the character of the saint or suggests the contrast of opposing qualities, or the allegorical combat between good and evil. It is said of St. Anthony the hermit, " Born of a noble stock, adorned with the gift of God, he was conspicuous in virtues. He sought the caves of the desert lest the world with its riches deceive him, thrust into the midst of sins." [2] St. Benedict inspires this prayer:

---

[1] *Dilecto regi virtutum*, H.M., line 7 (St. Katherine). *Odas hac in die laetas*, S.M., line 20 (St. Katherine). *Caelum, mare, tellus*, W.T., line 10 (St. Birinus). *Laude celebret vox*, W.T., line 14 (St. Ethelwold). *Exsultemus et laetemur*, Y.M., lines 9, 10 (St. John of Beverley).

[2] *In hac die laetabunda*, S.M., stanza 2.

" Grant, we pray thee, O God, mighty ruler, that our faith
may resist sins and aid us to a desire for the virtues in purity
of heart." [1]   It was St. Martin who " caused the seeds of
the virtues to grow where sins had been." [2]   He also participated in the struggle with evil.   " With these weapons,
conquering the ranks of Tartarus, in his eagerness for the
virtues, he achieved the glorious joys of heaven." [3]   St.
Thomas of Hereford is implored for aid in the good fight.
" Surround us, O Thomas, far-famed leader, with thy de-
fenses, graciously preserving thy hard pressed servants." [4]

The conception of the saints as warriors of God and spiritual leaders, already familiar from hymns in the Common
of Saints, is greatly expanded in the Proper of Saints. Hymn
after hymn contains the familiar expressions *miles fortis,
miles gloriosus, bellator inclitus, miles mirabilis,* and *miles
Christi* applied to individuals.   The evidence on this point
seems overwhelming.[5]   Again fortitude is the accompaniment of the Christian warrior, displayed by men and women
alike.   St. Vincent is an " indomitable witness " for God.
" He stands firm in torments, unshakable in constancy." [6]
St. Katherine " despises the terrors of martyrdom." [7]   A
new challenge to courage on the part of the saint, is offered
by the hardships of the missionary life.   St. Augustine of

---

[1] *Christe, sanctorum decus,* D.H., stanza 17.

[2] *Fratres unanimes foedere, Anal. Hymn.,* L, no. 154, lines 15, 16.

[3] *Promere chorda iam conetur,* W.T., line 4.

[4] *Summi regis in honore,* H.M., lines 7, 8.

[5] *In hac die laetabunda,* S.M., line 10 (St. Anthony). *Christi miles
gloriosus,* S.B., line 1 (St. Vincent). *Bellator armis inclitus, Anal.
Hymn.,* LI, no. 176 (St. Martin). *Magnus miles mirabilis,* D.H., line 1
(St. Cuthbert). *Voto voce cordis oris,* Y.M., line 22 (St. William of
York).

[6] *Beate martyr prospera, Anal. Hymn.,* L, no. 35, line 11; *Christo
canamus dei,* Y.M., line 16.

[7] *Odas hac in die laetas,* S.M., line 10.

Canterbury overcame them.   " No terror of his trackless
course daunted him, nor did the angry waters cool the ardor
of his advance." [1]

All the forms of restraint, self-control and temperance are
manifested in the lives of individual saints.   The negative
aspects of the ascetic life are shown in fasting and abstinence.
St. Anthony the hermit is " weakened by fasting."   St. Gen-
evieve " subdues the flesh by fasting "; St. Ethelwold " by
watches and much fasting ".[2]   The life of renunciation and
poverty is lauded.   This example was set by St. Anthony,
St. Martin, St. Cuthbert, St. Roch and many others.   In the
case of St. Martin, the contrast is made between poverty and
true riches.   " Behold, this man, poor and lowly, enters
heaven rich." [3]   In the long line of saints from St. Anthony
the hermit to the bishops of the later Middle Ages, that ideal
of poverty is confirmed, of which the life of Jesus was the
ultimate inspiration.   Its social meaning has already been indicated and no further discussion is necessary at this point.

Purity of heart and life is highly praised in the lives of
individual saints.   St. Nicholas was " a stranger to and im-
mune from all wantonness." [4]   St. Ethelbert and St. Thomas
of Hereford receive praises in terms similar to those of St.
John the Evangelist.[5]   The quality of purity, for which St.
Ethelbert was distinguished, was greatly lauded in connection
with his cult, already mentioned.   Purity is a condition to
the performance of miracles in the lives of St. John of

---

[1] *Aveto placidis*, D.H., lines 22-25.

[2] *In hac die laetabunda*, S.M., line 25; *Genovefae solemnitas*, S.M., lines
21, 22; *Dies sacra dies ista*, W.T., line 7.

[3] *In hac die laetabunda*, S.M., stanza 2; *Pater verbum eructavit*, Y.M.,
lines 7, 8; *In honorem salvatoris*, S.M., stanza 3b; *Rex Christe Martini
decus*, Anal. Hymn., L, no. 199, lines 9, 10.

[4] *Congaudentes exultemus*, S.M., line 6.

[5] *Laudes deo decantemus*, H.M., stanza 3; (St. Ethelbert); *Gaude mater
ecclesia cum canticis*, H.B., line 5 (St. Thomas of Hereford).

Beverley and of St. Wilfrid. Of the former it is said, "The saint praying with pure heart, gave health to the dying in the midst of a wondering throng." [1] Of the latter we learn, "What he merited on earth, he made clear in the world by his countless miracles which Christ manifested in the powers of him who desired to please his master, without stain." [2]

In St. Katherine is met the favorite among the Virgin Patronesses of the church and the type of the conventual ideal. There is no more appealing personality in the whole galaxy of martyrs, dear to the Middle Ages, than St. Katherine, if one may judge by the devotion she has commanded and the wide extent of her influence. England boasted eighty dedications in her honor besides many wayside chapels, as contrasted with twenty-six dedications to all the other virgin martyrs combined. Three out of every four counties possessed a church dedicated to her and many localities received her name as a memorial of the veneration with which their inhabitants regarded her.[3]

Following the liturgy which celebrates her praises, or the narrative in the *Golden Legend,* we discover that Katherine, daughter of King Costus of Alexandria, was a princess distinguished for beauty, learning and faith. Ascending the throne after her father's death, she began a strange and adventurous career of which her mystic marriage to the Child Jesus was the opening episode. Then came her disputation with the fifty wise men, her sufferings at the hands of the persecutor Maxentius, during which she miraculously escaped torture by the wheel, her death by the sword and, finally, her translation to Mt. Sinai and burial by angel ministrants.[4]

[1] *Gaude mater ecclesia in filiorum gloria,* Y.M., lines 31-33.

[2] *Salvatoris clementiae,* Y.M., stanza 4.

[3] F. Arnold-Forster, *Studies in Church Dedications* (London: Skeffington & Son, 1899), I, pp. 105, 117-121.

[4] *Golden Legend,* VII, p. 2 et seq.

In the eighth century her cult was already firmly established
in the East where she with St. Barbara and St. Margaret
was venerated among the chief Grecian virgin martyrs.[1]
In the eleventh century her relics were brought to Rouen by
Simeon, a monk of Sinai, and during the period of the
Crusades which immediately followed, a great impetus was
given to the cult.[2]   If crusaders carried her fame westward,
as Simeon had carried her relics, they were by no means her
exclusive devotees.   Guildsmen who used the wheel in their
trades adopted her cult.   Theologians, philosophers, orators
and students sought the aid of the virgin scholar.[3]   She
was immortalized in art, crowned with the three aureoles;
white for the virgin, green for the doctor, red for the martyr.
A favorite pose in sculpture and glass, is that of the maiden
with crown and palm or wheel trampling upon Maxentius.
The painters of the fifteenth century loved to portray the
marriage scene.   Fra Angelico, Memling, Correggio, Rubens,
Titian and Murillo all painted it.   Nor was St. Katherine
overlooked by writers of miracle plays as is attested by the
presentation of her story in dramatic form in England,
France and the Empire by the fourteenth century.[4]   In the
case of St. Katherine, art, legend, drama and hymns are
supplementary.   One of the hymns to her, *Odas hac in die
laetas,* offers a fairly long version of the legend, stressing
the learning and fortitude of the saint.   In *Aeternae virgo
memoriae* the thought is centered upon her mystic union.

Justice, which so far has appeared as a virtue of the
apostles, is now seen in the lives of other saints, chiefly those
who held positions of administrative leadership, among them

[1] A. M. Jameson, *Sacred and Legendary Art*, pp. 465-8.

[2] Abbé H. Brémond, *Sainte Catherine d'Alexandrie* (Paris: Laurens,
no date), p. 12.

[3] Brémond, *ibid.*, p. 62.

[4] W. Creizenach, *Geschichte des neueren Dramas*, I, pp. 95, 125.

St. Martin, St. Cuthbert, St. Benedict, St. Edmund, St. Thomas (Becket), St. William of York and St. Thomas of Hereford. The only person, aside from those of acknowledged prestige, who is called *just* in the hymns for the Proper of Saints, is Simeon, who received the Infant Jesus in the temple. This is doubtless a reflection of Luke 2 : 25 where Simeon is referred to as *just,* possibly in the Old Testament sense of *righteous,* while the saints mentioned above are thought of as displaying justice in their functions of authority.[1]

Prudence is attributed to St. Ethelwold as follows: " He prudently disbursed the sacred talents ",[2] a sentence which throws considerable light upon the virtue as it was understood at the time, by reference to the parable of the talents (Matthew 25 : 14-30).

Faith, a leading virtue in the hymns for saints in general, is an invariable characteristic in the praises of St. Agnes, St. Agatha, St. Denis, St. Laurence, St. Benedict, the English saints and many others.[3]

Hope, which so often refers to one powerful to save, is found in its ordinary meaning in the praise of saints. St. Winifred is described as " firm in faith, joyous in hope, holy

---

[1] *Sacerdotem Christi Martinum,* S.M., line 16 (St. Martin) ; *Pater verbum eructavit,* Y.M., lines 1-3 (St. Cuthbert) ; *Christe sanctorum decus,* D.H., line 37 (St. Benedict) ; *Omnis fidelium ecclesia,* H.M., line 7 (St. Edmund) ; *Iacet granum oppressum palea,* S.P., line 2 (St. Thomas Becket) ; *Coetus noster jocundetur,* Y.M., line 6 (St. William of York) ; *Magnae lucem caritatis,* H.M., line 21 (St. Thomas of Hereford) ; *Quod chorus vatum,* S.B., lines 9, 10 (Simeon).

[2] Cited, chap. IV, p. 126.

[3] *Agnes beatae virginis, Anal. Hymn.,* L, no. 11, stanza 3 (St. Agnes) ; *Martyris ecce dies Agathae, Anal. Hymn.,* LI, no. 134, lines 5, 6 (St. Agatha) ; *Gaude prole Graecia,* H.M., line 47 (St. Denis) ; *Laurea clara laetantem,* W.T., line 13 (St. Laurence) ; *Sancti meriti Benedicti,* W.T., line 8 (St. Benedict) ; *Spe mercedis et coronae,* Y.M., line 5 (St. Thomas Becket) ; *Caelum, mare, tellus,* W.T., line 13 (St. Birinus).

in act, pure in mind." [1]   The hope of salvation is also felt
to be a virtue, as it was undoubtedly regarded by medieval
teachers.[2] " The saints, reared in this faith, comforted by
hope, did not fear to suffer." [3] " In the hope of a reward
and crown, Thomas (Becket) stood suffering, obedient unto
death." [4]

Love, third and greatest of the theological virtues, is a
synonym for saintliness.   Like purity, it is evidenced by the
performance of miracles.   " The many miracles (of St.
Armagillus) prove his sanctity and fervent love." [5]   Among
others who are praised for this virtue are St. Benedict and
St. Ethelwold.[6]

Turning to virtues not included in the list of the seven
principal virtues, obedience is mentioned three times.   St.
Agatha " binds the commands of God to her heart." [7]   St.
Benedict teaches that the commands of God must be obeyed
and a hymn for St. Thomas of Hereford requires a " will
swift to obey." [8]

Generosity is a virtue highly commended.   Like humility,
which is the opposite of pride, generosity is the opposite of
avarice.   It is natural to think in terms of contrast, and to
place good and evil characteristics in opposing groups.   Two
of the deadly sins, namely *luxuria* and *acedia* may be attacked by *temperantia* and *fortitudo*.   Two more, namely,

[1] *Virgo vernans velut rosa*, S.M., stanza 1b.

[2] *Vide* John de Burgh, *Pupilla oculi*, p. clxiiii, *Spes est certa expectatio futurae beatitudinis ex dei gratia.*

[3] *Novi plausus incrementum*, H.M., stanza 11.

[4] *Spe mercedis et coronae*, Y.M., lines 1-3.

[5] *Corde lingua mente tota*, S.M., stanza 1b.

[6] *Christe sanctorum decus*, D.H., line 15 (St. Benedict); *Dies sacra dies ista*, W.T., line 8 (St. Ethelwold).

[7] *Martyris ecce dies Agathae, Anal. Hymn.*, LI, no. 134, line 8.

[8] *Christe sanctorum decus*, D.H., lines 20-22; *Novi plausus incrementum*, H. M., stanza 17a.

superbia and *avaritia,* call logically for the praise of *humilitas* and *largitas.* Probably this is the explanation of the praise of St. Laurence and St. Nicholas in particular, for the virtue of generosity.

The legend of St. Laurence contrasts the avarice of the persecutor Decius, the Roman usurper, with the generosity of the saint in a most dramatic way. The medieval version of the story as recounted in the *Golden Legend,* runs thus: Pope Sixtus II, it appears, had concealed the treasures of the church of Rome from Decius, fearing their confiscation. He then entrusted them to Laurence the Deacon to be expended for the churches and for the poor. This done, Laurence was brought before Decius. "And Decius said to him: 'Where be the treasures of the church, which we well know that thou hast hid?' And he answered not. Wherefore he delivered him to Valerianus the provost to the end that he should show the treasures and do sacrifice to the idols, or to put him to death by divers torments."[1] Citations from the hymns now become intelligible. "The avaricious Decius, tricked, gives way to lamentation. He makes ready the flames of vengeance."[2] "Laurence is summoned before the king and the hidden treasures of the church are mentioned. But he does not yield to flatteries nor is he weakened by the torments of his avaricious persecutor." The treasures of the church which were entrusted to St. Laurence were not hoarded but given to the poor. "A minister of love, he gives to the throng of poor abundant supplies for their needs."[3]

The popularity of the cult of St. Laurence and the wide currency given to tales of his martyrdom and miracles must have invested Decius with an importance even greater than

---

[1] *Golden Legend,* IV, p. 212.

[2] *Apostolorum supparem, Anal. Hymn.,* L, no. 16, lines 27, 28.

[3] *Stola jocunditatis,* S.M., verses 8, 9; *ibid.,* verse 11.

that which he had already as a typical Roman persecutor. Relics of the saint are said to have been sent to Northumbria in the Anglo-Saxon period, and many churches dedicated to him date from early times.   Yorkshire possessed eighteen of the 250 dedications throughout England.   Both facts point to a flourishing cult, especially in the northern section of the country.

St. Nicholas, who, like St. Laurence, occupied a position of high favor in the medieval period,[1] was distinguished by a generosity which is reflected in hymns extolling his virtues. " He was characterized by great compassion, and he conferred many benefits upon the oppressed.   Through his aid the shame of the maidens is removed by a gift of gold, and the poverty of their father is relieved." [2]   The hymn from which this stanza has been selected recounts several incidents from the legend of the saint, but none was more popular than this, the tale of the poverty-stricken father and his three daughters whose needs were supplied by St. Nicholas.   To each of the girls a dowry was furnished to enable her to enjoy honorable marriage.[3]   If the testimony of art is to be credited, the theme of the charity of St. Nicholas is in general the most favored of all his virtuous acts.   The bishop is commonly represented with three golden balls illustrating the three purses given to the dowerless girls.   In fact it is one of the common symbols by which to identify the figure of the saint.[4]   Additional weight is given to the theory that

[1] There were 437 dedications in England in honor of St. Nicholas, representing every county. *Vide* F. Bond, *Dedications and Patron Saints of English Churches*, pp. 17, 66; F. Arnold-Forster, *Studies in Church Dedications*, I, pp. 489-500.

[2] *Congaudentes exultemus*, S.M., stanza 3.

[3] *Golden Legend*, II, 109 *et seq.*   For a discussion of this hymn, *vide* H. O. Taylor, *Mediaeval Mind* (New York: Macmillan Co., 1914), II, 242.

[4] For illustrations of the life of St. Nicholas *vide* F. Bond, *op. cit.*, p. 26; A. Marguillier, *Saint Nicolas* (Paris: Laurens, no date), *passim.* Note especially the pictures by Fra Angelico, pp. 11, 21, 25, 43, 56.

St. Nicholas is thought of as a type of generosity by Dante's use of the legend. The spirit who celebrates the largess of St. Nicholas teaches the avaricious man in Purgatory how to purify the soul from the stains of his besetting sin.[1]

Mention has been made from time to time of the notorious persecutors of the martyrs. The sins conventionally attributed to this group have been further emphasized in the condemnation of Maxentius who was responsible for the death of St. Katherine, and of Decius who persecuted St. Laurence. Quintianus, a Roman official in Sicily and the foe of St. Agatha and other Christians, must now be added to the list. "Quintianus, tyrant of Sicily, hearing of the virgin's fame, began to rage with envy."[2] Such phrases are by this time becoming wearisome through repetition. The novel development along this line is furnished by the transfer of the familiar epithets to the enemies of later medieval saints, among them St. Thomas of Canterbury. "The fury of the soldiers rages, as he is sacrificed at the sacred altar, a holy victim."[3] In the hymns which honor St. William of York there are a number of references to envy. Inasmuch as the circumstances of his life are well known it may help toward an understanding of what *invidia* meant to people of the Middle Ages when it was associated, not with the Roman persecutors but with their own contemporaries. "Deposed by the deceit of envious men, he nevertheless gave praise and thanks to God. Living a life of exile for seven years, he endured hardship to his soul's health."[4] "Envy pursuing thee and injustice overcoming thee, at length thou dost suffer exile."[5]

---

[1] Dante, *Purgatorio*, Canto XX.

[2] *Agathae sacrae virginis, Anal. Hymn.*, LI, no. 135, stanza 2.

[3] *Spe mercedis et coronae*, Y.M., line 7.

[4] *Plaudat chorus plebs laetetur*, Y.M., stanzas 5, 6.

[5] *Regi Christo applaudat ecclesia*, Y.M., stanza 7.

William Fitzherbert, an English nobleman, formerly treasurer and canon of York, was elected archbishop in 1142 in spite of the strong opposition of the Cistercians of Fountains Abbey. The minority believed that William had gained the election through bribery and royal influence. After much dispute in England, the case was taken to Rome where the Cistercians, headed by Richard, abbot of Fountains Abbey and powerfully supported by Bernard of Clairvaux, appealed against William. Innocent II decided that if the charges could be cleared away, William could be consecrated. This was done in 1143. The pallium was sent to England by Lucius, successor of Innocent II but William failed to claim it promptly. Accordingly, when Lucius died and Eugenius III was made pope, the pallium was returned to Rome and the charges against William renewed through the determined efforts of Bernard. A second time William journeyed to Rome but without success for he was suspended on a technicality, 1147. A voluntary exile, William went first to Sicily, then to Winchester where he cultivated the ascetic life. The year 1153 was marked by the death of his chief foes, Bernard and Eugenius III. Appearing as a suppliant before the new pope, Anastasius IV, William was restored to his rights. He entered York in May, 1154, but lived only one month to enjoy his honors. The bitterness of his foes pursued him to the very end, for rumor has it that he died of poison which had been placed deliberately in the eucharistic chalice. William was canonized in 1227.[1] Without entering into the merits of the case, this story of medieval church politics is full of human interest. Just as it stands, it throws a strong light upon the sin of *invidia* as interpreted by the supporters of St. William. St. Bernard evidently understood the matter quite differently, which reminds the student

[1] The foregoing account is taken from the *Dictionary of National Biography* where full references from the sources may be found.

of ethics how often moral judgment depends upon the point of view.

It is fitting to close the recital of the virtues of this group of non-biblical saints with the praises of St. Osmund, to whom the English church owes so great a debt. *Gaudeamus Messia,* the sequence which contains the list of his many virtues, is peculiarly interesting. Osmund is revealed as a saint who possessed all the seven principal virtues and repudiated all the seven deadly sins. " Prudent, strong, temperate, sturdy in faith and hope, he is pre-eminent for justice. Moreover, he excels in love, and by these God-given arms he conquered his sins. Pride, wrath, envy, avarice, sloth, gluttony, the practice of arms and the chase, he strikes down, slays, destroys, drives off, puts to flight, abolishes and repels, a stainless knight." [1] Here is the spiritual knight in full panoply, master of himself and of his foes.

The value of the objective ideal, already so strongly felt in hymns used for the Common of Saints, is greatly reinforced by the definite challenge to imitate the virtues of a particular saint. A poet who praises St. Benedict, addresses the people of the heavenly courts whom he thinks of as securing celestial favor by following St. Benedict's example. " Pray to Benedict our patron, that ye may gain celestial favor, together with eternal salvation, by following his holy example." [2] St. Ethelwold has set an example for the English. " As bishop he taught the Angles by his shining example, how to achieve the lofty heights of the heavenly court." [3] St. William of York is a model for imitation. " His life is the pattern of a pure and fruitful life, and a theme for praise." [4] The theme of emulation is employed

[1] *Gaudeamus Messia*, S.M., stanzas 4, 5.
[2] *Arce superna cuncta*, W.T., lines 4, 5.
[3] *Laude celebret vox*, W.T., line 6.
[4] *Voto, voce, cordis oris*, Y.M., lines 3-5.

by one who praised St. Thomas of Hereford with double
force.   Let the worshipper, he implies, imitate the great
bishop of Hereford, just as he, the bishop, followed the example of St. Thomas the Apostle and St. Thomas Becket.
" Let us in united praises reverence Thomas the bishop and
strive to imitate him.—For love of poverty he follows the
Apostle; for the fervor of his love he is joined to the Martyr.
In the faith of his confession he follows the first Thomas,
and in his eagerness for suffering he is a companion of the
second." [1]   In view of the fact that specific virtues are
named in this hymn and that historic personages of medieval
England are concerned this is no vague generalization.   We
know that, for instance, Thomas Becket was greatly rever-
enced in the diocese of Hereford.   Surely it is a fair inference
to suppose that the desirability of imitating a saintly example
was an idea rather generally entertained.   The evidence of
collects which appear in the liturgy for the festivals of saints
supports this view, although the intercessory idea is much
more important.   The conventionl form of the petition is
represented by two phrases, the former from the liturgy in
honor of St. Paul, the latter from that of St. Philip and St.
James.   " Grant that we may approach thee through the
example of him, whose conversion we celebrate this day; "
" That we may be instructed by the examples of those in
whose merits we rejoice." [2]   A particular virtue of St.
Agnes is to be imitated in the next prayer.   " Grant that we
may follow her in the example of holy intercourse, just as
we venerate her in this office." [3]   Imitation and intercession
are often mingled.   " Grant to us in mercy, entrance to the
heavenly kingdom through the intercession of him by whose
example we are instructed in righteous living." [4]

[1] *Magnae lucem caritatis*, H.M., lines 4-6, 7-12.

[2] S.B., III, 110; S.B., III, 267.

[3] S.B., III, 125.   [4] S.B., I, ccclxvii.

There can be no reasonable doubt that the medieval church taught both by prayer and hymn the necessity for cultivating the great virtues which were embodied in saintly examples. Forces were thus released, the far-reaching effects of which in society it is impossible to measure. When the worshipper has yielded to the influence of an exalted character, he has ranged himself upon the positive side in the struggle between good and evil. In taking his place with those whose virtues have uplifted humanity, he has justified the veneration of the saints who have inspired him. Indeed, this is the chief significance of such veneration for the student of the legends of the saints as Father Delehaye has made clear in an eloquent passage.[1]

Hymns for the Proper of Saints in the English collections reflect the medieval cults with beauty and restraint. A lofty conception is present, generally speaking, both of the character of the saint and of man's duty in relation to the ideal which has been set up before him. Finally, the ideal itself is sharply defined in terms of virtues already familiar in hymns for other parts of the liturgy and in the legends of the saints, as they were known in biography, in drama and in art.

The hymns for the principal saints' days which are included in the Proper of Saints have already been mentioned. The festivals of the Virgin and of the leading saints account for almost all of them. There remain chiefly, the hymns used in the liturgy for the feasts of the Transfiguration, the Name of Jesus, and All Saints. Like the hymns for Easter, Ascension, and Trinity, those used for the Transfiguration are primarily devoted to praise, and are not concerned with conduct. The feast of the Name of Jesus is also one of praise,

[1] H. Delehaye, *Legends of the Saints* (London: Longmans, Green & Co., 1907), pp. 229-231; translated from *Les Légendes hagiographiques* (Bruxelles: Polleunis et Ceuterick, 1905).

but the hymns reveal a subjective attitude which is absent in those for the Transfiguration. The best known of this group is, of course, *Jesu dulcis memoria,* which has been treasured for centuries by Christians of every variety of religious opinion, and requires no comment here. It illustrates the contemplative aspect of monastic life which came to be as influential in hymnology as did the ascetic phase.

With the hymns for All Saints the culmination of the praises of the heavenly throng is reached. Resembling the hymns for the Common of Saints in their inclusiveness, these pieces are more elaborate in their mention of the ranks of heaven. A conventional arrangement is followed, in which the Virgin stands first, then the angelic hierarchies, then patriarchs, prophets, apostles, martyrs, confessors, virgins and churchmen, whose prayers and protection are sought. Coming toward the close of the liturgical year, All Saints Day fittingly gathers up the praises of the long line of saints who have been separately honored during the preceding months. The Sarum liturgy for All Saints includes a noble sequence, *Christo inclito candida.* As might be expected there is recognition for the leadership of the saints and the potency of their defense. " Grant us brave hearts and strength of body that the weapons of holiness may fitly conquer the foe." [1] Of the Virgin, purity is besought. " Keep our souls and bodies pure." [2] Another piece for All Saints closes with this prayer : " Let us guard our love, let us hold fast purity, let us render again our faith, stainless and secure." [3] The four great virtues, courage and purity, love and faith are left uppermost in the thought of the worshipper, as the cherished virtues to be cultivated through the power of saintly example. Conse-

[1] *Christo inclito candida,* S.M., line 12.
[2] *Ibid.,* line 16.
[3] *Gaudet clemens dominus,* W.T., lines 24, 25.

quently, the considerations which are suggested by the festival of All Saints serve as a fitting conclusion to the discussion of hymns found in the Proper of Saints.

Before summarizing the ethical ideals which are presented in the hymns for the third and last section of the liturgy, in which the seven sins and seven virtues of medieval thought are so prominent, it will be necessary to make a final digression into other fields of religious opinion. During the period in which the hymns honoring the saints were greatly multiplied, the lists of sins and virtues reached their completed form. The standard was constantly appearing in every variety of expression, testifying to a general and widespread acquaintance with the ideas which it implied. In harmony with the developments outside of hymnology, the seven virtues and the seven sins are more clearly defined in the liturgy for the Proper of Saints. The ideas generally current at this time should be understood, if the reflection of those ideas is to be studied in hymns or a comparison of the related forms of expression is to be made.

Medieval opinion upon the subject of seven deadly sins, which had been varying for centuries, was finally expressed in permanent form by Peter Lombard (d. 1160?). Throwing his influence upon the side of Gregorian tradition, he confirmed the list beginning with *superbia* (*inanis gloria*) and ending with *acedia*.[1] Hugh of St. Victor, (d. 1141), his contemporary, and a leader of mysticism in France, also approved Gregory's list which was best fitted to the allegorical and symbolic treatment of religious ideas, at that time becoming more common. In the *Allegoriae in Novum Testamentum,* a work attributed to Hugh of St. Victor, the subject is discussed with the following definitions of the sins: " Pride is love of one's own superiority. Envy is jealousy of another's happiness. Wrath is the irrational excitement

[1] Peter Lombard, *Sententiae*, ii, *Dist.* 42, 8 (PL, cxcii, 753).

of the mind. Sloth is the aversion to inner goodness.
Avarice is the immoderate eagerness for possessions. Gluttony is too great fondness for eating. Impurity is the immoderate desire for the satisfaction of sensuality." [1]   As an
illustration of this author's treatment in general it may be
noted that he takes up in one place the various petitions of the
Lord's prayer, pointing out the efficacy of each one in opposing a different specific sin from the list of seven.[2]   In addition to the writings doubtfully attributed to Hugh of St.
Victor, his authenticated works contain many references to
the subject identical in spirit with the ones cited above.[3]

In the thirteenth century Thomas Aquinas and Bonaventura definitely incorporated the list into the accepted theology of the medieval church.   Among others, Alexander of
Hales, Caesarius of Heisterbach, William of Auvergne,
Grosseteste of Lincoln and Vincent of Beauvais contributed
further discussion of the subject.[4]

A canon of the Fourth Lateran Council of 1215 made
annual confession obligatory.[5]   Perhaps this date may afford
some indication of the period in which the standard of seven

---

[1] *Superbia = amor propriae excellentiae, invidia = livor alienae felici-
tatis, ira = irrationabilis perturbatio mentis, acedia = fastidium interni
boni, avaritia = immoderata habendi cupiditas, gula = nimius edendi ap-
petitus, luxuria = immoderatum desiderium explendae libidinis.*   In
Exegetica dubia; Allegoriae in N. T., ii, 3 (PL, clxxv, 774).

[2] Hugh of St. Victor, *ibid.,* ii, 6 (PL, clxxv, 777).

[3] Hugh of St. Victor, *De fructibus carnis et spiritus* (PL, clxxvi, 997
et seq.) ; *De sacramentis,* ii, 13 (PL, clxxvi, 525 *et seq.*) ; *Summa sententiarum,* iii, 16 (PL, clxxvi, 113).

[4] O. Zöckler, *Das Lehrstück von den sieben Hauptsünden,* p. 80;
Alexander of Hales, *Summa universae theologiae,* II, clii-clxi; Caesarius
of Heisterbach, *Dialogus miraculorum,* IV, *de tentatione*; William of
Auvergne, *De vitiis et peccatis*; Vincent of Beauvais, *Speculum doc-
trinale,* V, vi.

[5] For the text *vide* C. J. Hefele-Leclercq, *Histoire des Conciles* (Paris:
Letouzey, 1913), V, 2e partie, pp. 1349-50.

sins became generally acknowledged, because of its intimate connection with the sacrament of penance. The use of the adjective " deadly " in connection with the list of seven sins seems to have originated from the inclusive character which the theologians had by that time attributed to them.[1] The thirteenth century is also the period of origin of the *Summae Confessorum,* the juristic character of which has already been mentioned. The *Summae* were technical works for the guidance of the confessor in questions relating to the deadly sins as well as other problems of conscience.[2] The names of Robert of Flamesbury, Raymond of Pennaforte, William of Rennes, John of Freiburg, Burchard of Strasburg and William of Cayeux are representatives of the early thirteenth century group. The first mentioned, Robert of Flamesbury, devoted the fourth book of his *Summa* to a detailed discussion of all forms of sin, first of all to the seven deadly sins. At the close of the book he recommended penances to be imposed.

The seven deadly sins obviously formed a convenient standard for both the confessor and the penitent whose recollection was strengthened by the use of the acrostic or memory word *Saligia,* formed by the initial letters of the words *superbia, avaritia, luxuria, ira, gula, invidia* and *acedia.* It is first recorded by the canonist Henricus Ostiensis, Bishop of Ostia (1271), who apparently considers it familiar already. He says,

> *Dat septem vicia,*
> *Dictio saligia.*[3]

[1] H. C. Lea, *History of Auricular Confession and Indulgences* (Philadelphia: Lea, 1896), II, pp. 236-239.

[2] J. Dietterle, " Die Summae Confessorum ", *Zeitschrift für Kirchengeschichte,* XXIV (1903), 353-363.

[3] Henricus Ostiensis, *Summa s. Tractatus de poenitentiis et remissione,* v, 38; cited by O. Zöckler, *Das Lehrstück von den sieben Hauptsünden,* p. 69.

As time went on manuals of instruction for parish priests were used. They must have been common enough from the period when private confession became the general practice of the church. About one hundred years after Henricus Ostiensis, an important English work appeared, *Pupilla Oculi*, by John de Burgh, partly a compendium of legal information and partly a parish manual. The general character of this work may be understood from the citations which have been used in the preceding pages. The definitions which De Burgh gives of the deadly sins are very similar to those of Hugh of St. Victor, quoted above. Each one is carefully analyzed and separated into its various forms, leaving no doubt in the mind of the reader as to its implications and results.

John Myrc, canon of Lilleshall (c. 1400), an English moralist, produced a manual in poetic form, verses 1085-1414 of which are significantly entitled *De modo inquirendi de VII peccatis mortalibus,* while verses 1667-1736 recommend appropriate penances.[1]

The work of Guilhelmus Peraldus which must now be noted, serves as a convenient transition from the writings of the theologians to the sermons of the medieval preachers who were carrying to the common people everywhere the principles of right living. The great impetus given to popular preaching by the crusades resulted throughout western Europe in a general increase of sermons in the vernacular, even before the mendicant orders consecrated their efforts to the task of preaching.[2] With the coming of the friars vernacular sermons were common enough. Peraldus or Perrault (d. 1275), of whose life very little is known, was a

---

[1] "Concerning the method of inquiring about the seven mortal sins." J. Myrc, *Instructions for Parish Priests*, E.E.T.S., vol. 31.

[2] E. C. Dargan, *History of Preaching* (N. Y.: Armstrong, 1905), I, p. 184.

noted Dominican preacher of Lyons, the author of a book entitled *Summa de Virtutibus et Vitiis* or *Somme des Vertues et des Vices*.[1] In this practical guide he often describes the sins figuratively, likening them to animals and other objects of nature. Immensely influential because of its simplicity, the book became the ancestor, so to speak, of a series upon the same subject both French and English, among them *Le Manuel des Péchés* by William of Waddington, later translated by Robert Mannyng of Brunne under the title *Handlyng Synne;* and *Somme des Vices et Vertues* or *Somme le Roi* by the Dominican Lorens, later translated by Dan Michel of Northgate under the title *Ayenbite of Inwyt*.[2] In his work Peraldus added the " sin of the tongue " to the usual list of seven sins.[3] Books like these, written as handbooks for the preacher rather than in the spirit of a theological treatise, became extremely popular. They are indicative of what was actually said in the sermons which were built upon the suggestions given in the manual. Combined with a supply of illustrative exempla such as Jacques de Vitry (1160-1240) had provided for the use of preachers, they reveal to a certain extent the mental background of those congregations to whom they were ultimately addressed.

Several collections exist of such illustrative stories used by preachers.[4] If grouped about the theme of the seven sins

---

[1] *Hist. Litt. de la France*, XIX, pp. 307-316; *Bibliothek der katholischen Pädagogik* (Freiburg im Breisgau: Herder, 1890), III, p. 212.

[2] For this series consult G. R. Owst, *Preaching in Medieval England*, p. 290.

[3] *peccatum linguae.*

[4] Jacques de Vitry, *Exempla*, edited by T. F. Crane, Folk Lore Soc. Pub. (London: Bell, 1904), vol. xxvi; Étienne de Bourbon, *Tractatus de diversis materiis praedicabilibus*, edited by A. Lecoy de la Marche, *Anecdotes historiques* (Paris: Renouard, 1877); *Gesta Romanorum,* edited by Swan and Hooper (London: Bell, 1904); J. A. Mosher, *The Exemplum in the Early Religious and Didactic Literature of England* (N. Y.: Col. Univ. Press, 1911).

and seven virtues the tales will be found to contain a large amount of material on this subject. The sin of avarice is evidently very abhorrent to Jacques de Vitry, who connects it with the practice of usury. Sometimes his tale appeals to fear. He tells of a usurer who provided that his money should be buried with him. Later when the grave was opened, demons were found filling the mouth of the corpse with red-hot coins. Sometimes he ridicules. He says that a certain rich miser kept a pie so long that when he finally set it before his guests the mice ran out of it. In another place Jacques de Vitry touches upon the whole group of sins as he preaches against the wickedness of tournaments, showing how all the seven mortal sins are committed by one who participates in them.[1]

Étienne de Bourbon (b. 1195), Dominican preacher and inquisitor, whose great work *Tractatus de diversis materiis praedicabilibus* contains a careful analysis of the seven deadly sins, classifies and illustrates them at the same time. Evidently an admirer of Jacques de Vitry, he not only follows his method but borrows many of his stories. Subdivisions of the sins are numerous, of which the analysis of pride may be taken as an illustration. Under the caption of *Pride* appear " concerning pride and its forms, vainglory, harmfulness of deceptive beauty or ornament, and physical superiority. Wherefore one should not betray pride in goods, ambition, hypocrisy, disobedience, stubbornness, irreverence and sacrilege toward person or place, violation of sacred feasts, presumption, heresy or superstition." The little tale which is intended to illuminate the subject of deceptive beauty has a double edge, showing how pride, as the author explains, harms both the sinner and others. A townswoman of Paris, beautified by feminine arts, appearing in a procession on a

[1] *Exempla*, CLXVIII, CLXXX, CXLI.

certain feast day, is followed with interest by her own husband without being recognized by him. Another tale for the discouragement of pride recounts the self-deception and disappointment of a clerk who counted on becoming a bishop, merely on the strength of a dream.[1]

English preachers are no exception to the rule when the favorite themes of virtues and vices are approached. " Once let the medieval homilist get astride of the vices, and then the virtues which ever accompany them, and he may be safely trusted to gallop to his conclusion." [2] References to the seven deadly sins made by John Waldeby (d. 1393), a popular Augustinian friar, and collected in a contemporary table, total fifty-six references to *avaritia,* thirty-three to *luxuria,* thirty-two to *superbia,* twenty-three to *invidia* and nineteen to *gula.*[3]

Of all thirteenth-century preachers the Franciscan Berthold of Regensburg may have been the most influential. He traveled widely, addressing all classes of persons. It has been estimated that his huge outdoor congregations numbered many thousands.[4] His sermons glow with fervor and are vital with the love of God, captivating the imagination of even the modern reader. To Berthold the accepted standard of the deadly sins was a reality in Christian experience. In one of his sermons he treats them in the old allegoric manner, identifying the seven with the enemies of Joshua in Canaan.

---

[1] A. Lecoy de la Marche, *op. cit.,* pp. 228, 224, 225.

[2] Owst, *op. cit.,* p. 322.

[3] Owst, *op. cit.,* pp. 322-323.

[4] Berthold von Regensburg, *Predigten,* edited by Pfeiffer and Strobl (Wien: Braumuller, 1862-1880).
The editors have assembled references for the sources for Berthold's life in vol. i, pp. xx-xxxii. The number of persons addressed by Berthold in various places, according to medieval authors, vary from 12,000 to 200,000. These totals, obviously highly exaggerated, may refer to all who heard him in one locality during his stay.

In other sermons he changes and amplifies the list, with ever fresh variety of treatment.   On these and other subjects Berthold spoke directly to the masses in terms which they could understand.   Therefore, his work is a valuable source from which to garner a harvest of popular ideals.[1]

Meantime the fusion of the seven principal virtues into one group had taken place, as a result of the belief that they were transmitted to men through the seven gifts of the Holy Spirit.   This belief has been explained in connection with the hymns for Pentecost.

During the thirteenth century Aquinas is the supreme exponent of the theology of the Christian virtues.[2]   Among those who wrote for a less learned group, Guilhelmus Peraldus gave equal attention to the virtues as to the sins in his work *Summa de Virtutibus et Vitiis* which has already been mentioned,—a treasure house for preachers and ascetics.

The authors of the *Summae Confessorum* and other manuals of the juristic type were insistent upon the exact definition and application of terms referring to the virtues, as well as to the sins.   John de Burgh in his manual *Pupilla Oculi* was most conscientious in his efforts to make plain the definitions of the various sins and virtues, supporting his statements by copious citations from the ancient philosophers, the Christian theologians or the Scriptures themselves.

The preachers of the Middle Ages were active in spreading the teachings of the church regarding the seven virtues.   They sought to impress upon their hearers the ideal of the virtues

---

[1] Pfeiffer, *ibid.*, XIII, *von 12 Scharn hern Jôsuê*; VI, *von ruofenden Sünden*; XV, *von den fremeden Sünden*; XXVII, *von fünf schedelîchen Sünden.*   Selections from the sermons of Berthold of Regensburg, translated into modern German, appear in E. Michael, *Geschichte des deutsche Volkes*, vol. i.   For other translations *vide* F. Göbel, *Die Missionspredigten des Franziskaners Berthold v. Regensburg* (Regensburg: Mainz, 1857).

[2] Aquinas, *Summa*, II, i, 61, 62.

in its symbolic form, ringing the changes upon the seven virtues, seven gifts, seven petitions of the Pater Noster, seven works of mercy, seven beatitudes, seven sacraments and seven deadly sins.[1] The *Tractatus* of Étienne de Bourbon is in reality a classification upon a large scale of the related aspects of the seven gifts, seven virtues and seven sins.

Berthold of Regensburg was fully as earnest in stressing the positive side of ethics and morality as he was in denouncing the deadly sins. He prefers the traditional list of virtues although he mentions others in some of his sermons.[2] The teaching value of the symbolic number was too great to permit of its disuse in favor of other systems especially when the weight of theological influence lay behind it.

Thus far medieval opinion upon the seven sins and seven virtues has been traced only in the works of theologians and preachers. It remains to consider briefly the reflection of the teaching in didactic poetry, popular tales, lives of saints, the drama and artistic representation.

Prudentius, it will be recalled, initiated the poetical treatment of the sins and virtues, employing the allegorical method in a most effective manner. Aldhelm (d. 709) became his imitator in an epic poem *De laude virginum*. He describes the struggle of man with sin and the conflict of virtues and vices. In the following century, Theodulphus of Orleans (c. 797), another imitator of Prudentius, took up the epic method but he did not complete his poem. Hermannus Contractus (d. 1054) contributed a poem, this time dramatic in character, *De octo vitiis principalibus,* upon the well-worn

---

[1] Aquinas approves the following adaptation of sacraments and virtues: Baptism corresponds to faith, extreme unction to hope, the eucharist to charity, ordination to prudence, penance to justice, matrimony to temperance, confirmation to fortitude. (*Summa*, III, 61, 1.)

[2] Pfeiffer, *Predigten*, XXVIII, *Von zwein unde vierzic Tugenden.*

theme.[1]   Alan of Lille completes the list of those who used the allegorical method, with his poem *Anticlaudianus*.[2]

In the borderland between the realms of religious and of secular literature may be placed the lives of saints.   From being regarded as pious tales they passed through a process of evolution which carried them into the field of romance. They are replete with incidents in which the various sins are repudiated or the virtues exemplified.   Another class of stories, in part secular, in part religious, is represented by the *Gesta Romanorum,* a collection of 181 tales which has been called " the most popular story book of the Middle Ages." [3] The preachers used the collection of tales, each of which is accompanied by a moral which explains the story in allegorical fashion.   Thirty-one of the stories refer to the seven sins or seven virtues in some way.   To quote no. XLVI, *Of Mortal Sins,* in full :

Julius relates that in the month of May a certain man entered a grove, in which stood seven beautiful trees in leaf.   The leaves so much attracted him, that he collected more than he had the strength to carry.   On this, three men came to his assistance, who led away both the man and the load beneath which he laboured.   As he went out he fell into a deep pit, and the extreme weight upon his shoulders sank him to the very bottom.

My beloved, the grove is the world, wherein are many trees, pleasant indeed to the eye, but putting forth only mortal sins. With these man loads himself.   The three men who brought assistance are the devil, the world, and the flesh; the pit is hell.[4]

The Canterbury Tales offer one of the best known illustra-

[1] O. Zöckler, *Tugendlehre*, pp. 126, 259-260, 265.

[2] Alanus de Insulis, *Anticlaudianus* (PL, ccx, 564-576).

[3] *Gesta Romanorum* edited by Swan and Hooper (London: Bell, 1904), p. v.

[4] *Gesta Romanorum, ibid.,* pp. 81, 82.

tions of the subject of virtues and sins in the *Persones Tale*, a homily, to be accurate, rather than a tale. The crowning work of medieval literature in any language, Dante's *Divina Commedia*, is itself a witness to the importance of the concept of seven sins and seven virtues for Dante incorporates them into the very substance of medieval religion. In his *Purgatorio* the poet describes the terraces for the seven deadly sins and in his *Paradiso* he expounds the theological virtues.[1]

The close and vital connection which exists between the liturgical drama of the Middle Ages and certain great medieval hymns has long been understood and carefully studied. The drama as a hand-maiden of the church in the great task of religious instruction, is also appreciated as one of the most potent of the objective methods of teaching that was employed. Both the liturgical and secular forms of the drama were genuinely popular, appealing to the tastes and the beliefs of those who witnessed them. No book of popular devotion, no prose or poetic writings upon religious subjects for the unlearned or indifferently educated, was more efficacious in attaining its desired end than the medieval drama.[2] Their authors share in common with those who wrote for the uncultured classes the credit of a real achievement.

When secular drama in England superseded the liturgical form it remained, therefore, a vehicle of popular religious instruction through the great Corpus Christi Cycles and the morality plays. The first English moralities were Paternoster Plays, which carried into the later medieval centuries the notion already explained, that the petitions of the Lord's Prayer were potent in combat with the deadly sins. Ac-

[1] Dante, *Divina Commedia*, Purgatorio, Canto X-XXVII. *Paradiso*, Canto XXIV, XXV, XXVI.

[2] L. Petit de Julleville, *Les Mysteres* (Paris: Hachette, 1880), vol. i, pp. 1, 2, 12; F. A. Gasquet, *Parish Life in Mediaeval England*, p. 250.

cordingly, the scenes are entitled " Pryde " and so forth, and
the underlying idea is the dramatization of the struggle between virtues and vices for the soul of man. Thus the allegory is transferred from the poetic to the dramatic medium
where it finds its most appropriate expression. Other
dramas devoted to the episodes of the Biblical narrative and
to the lives of saints have already been mentioned and their
importance in teaching the lessons of ethics, pointed out.

The expression of poetic and figurative ideas relating to
the sins and virtues is found in sculpture, painting and
stained glass as well as in the drama. Art is the paramount
expression of medieval life. It was neither imposed from
above nor did it originate in the patronage of political despots
nor merchant princes, except in pre-Renaissance Italy. It
was related in a peculiar way to life and popular thought.[1]
However one may evaluate the testimony of literature, the
testimony of art deserves close attention. It represents very
vividly the actual appropriation that had been made in daily
life of moral ideas, whatever their origin.

The figure of the tree with branches representing virtues
and vices growing from the root of love or of pride originated in the work attributed to Hugh of St. Victor. It
appears in the *Somme le Roi* of Lorens, in the *Desert of Religion* ascribed to Richard Rolle of Hampole and in the
Ayenbite of Inwyt.[2] Diagrams representing similar figures
were used in the illumination of manuscripts and were
painted on the walls of churches. Here the symbolic value
of the number seven is heightened by seven branches for each
of the seven sins or virtues.[3] The figurative representation

[1] Percy Dearmer in F. J. C. Hearnshaw, *Mediaeval Contributions to Modern Civilization* (London: Harrap, 1921), chap v, pp. 164-173.

[2] J. E. Wells, *Manual*, pp. 345-346; O. Zöckler, *Tugendlehre*, pp. 248, 255.

[3] E. L. Cutts, *Parish Priests and their People*, pp. 228-230.

by animal forms was employed by Herrad of Landsberg (d. 1195) whose virtues and vices were symbolized by knights mounted on animals, in her *Hortus deliciarum.* The struggle motive is also present. The conception of a ladder of virtues which appealed to other writers has been mentioned already.[1] The general method of representation in art, however, is by human figures, sometimes men in combat, sometimes merely contrasting figures, often women.

At Strasburg minster the fourteenth-century stained glass shows twelve figures of the virtues. The frescoes of Giotto and Andrea Pisano in the campanile at Florence represent the Seven Virtues with the Sacraments, Beatitudes and Works of Mercy. Giotto's frescoes in the Church of St. Maria dell'Arena at Padua show contrasting women's figures depicting the Seven Virtues and Seven Sins.[2]

The number seven suffers many changes in sculpture because the figures often fit into spaces corresponding to other groups. In the south portal of the Cathedral of Chartres there are twelve to match the figures of the twelve apostles. Amiens and Notre Dame (Paris) show twelve also. The form of depiction characteristic of the great French cathedral sculptures is that of the conflict or contrast. At Clermont, Tournay, Parthenay, Aulnay and Laon the numbers vary from six to eight. They are not always the usual groups, for sculpture necessarily lends itself to the treatment of exact counterparts rather than to a more abstract form of synthesis. In certain respects the Laon sculptures are the most interesting because the idea of exact counterparts leads the artist to Prudentius, although eight pairs of figures are used for the sake of symmetry, instead of the seven which Prudentius described. The Virtues in the form of armed women are represented at the moment of victory, triumphing over the

[1] O. Zöckler, *Tugendlehre*, pp. 251, 248-249.
[2] O. Zöckler, *Tugendlehre*, pp. 253-254.

Vices represented by figures of men cast down in subjection.
At Clermont the warring Virtues appear as feudal knights in
full armor engaged more strenuously in combat.   Thus the
different aspects of spiritual warfare are shown but the
favorite conception seems to be that of the final triumph
rather than the clash of antagonists which Prudentins immortalized.   So too, the ideal is depicted as accomplished and
within the powers of a struggling humanity buffetted by sin.[1]

Such was the development of the scheme of seven principal
virtues and seven deadly sins in the later medieval centuries.
Its manifold expressions are found in every form of literature
and of art, testifying not only to the widespread acquaintance
with the ideal which it embodied, but to its actual functioning
in society.   No wonder the hymn writers were concerned
with ethical teachings so pervasive, especially when they had
the authority of theological approval.

To summarize briefly the standards of conduct emphasized in hymns for the Proper of the Season, this third
division of the hymnal has made distinctive contributions to
the development and completion of the medieval ethical ideal.
The conception of the saint as the possessor of the virtues has
been made more striking by the creation of types of particular virtues, each one embodied in a single individual, like St.
Peter, the type of faith, or St. Stephen, the type of love.
Virtues which are the opposites of sins in the list of seven
sins, but for which there is no corresponding virtue in the
list of seven virtues, are greatly emphasized, namely, humility, the opposite of pride, and generosity, the opposite of

---

[1] For a fascinating treatment of this subject *vide* E. Mâle, *op. cit.*,
Livre III, *Le Miroir Moral*. For a description of the sculptures at Laon
vide L. Broche, *La Cathédrale de Laon* (Paris: *Laurens*, 1926), pp. 65-66.
For illustrations *vide* P. Vitry et G. Brière, *Documents de Sculpture
française du Moyen Age* (Paris: Longuet), Amiens, plate LIX; Chartres,
plate XLII; Notre Dame, plate XLVIII. Also E. Mâle, *ibid.*, Clermont,
pp. 127-128; Aulnay, p. 129.

avarice. Meekness, a virtue which is closely related to humility, is exalted in St. Andrew who becomes the type of that quality. Generosity is strongly commended by the example of St. Laurence and St. Nicholas. Indeed, the attack made upon the sins of pride and avarice by the positive method of inculcating humility, meekness and generosity is one of the most interesting phases of hymns which honor saints.

It would be difficult and perhaps impossible to demonstrate that virtues such as the cardinal virtues, which have a high social value, were increased in society through the veneration of saints. It is highly probable, however, that such was the case, and that hymns, side by side with other means of religious education, inspired men and women to the cultivation of ideal qualities in daily living. The direct injunction to imitate the virtues of the saint, which is characteristic of this group of hymns, points to a definite attempt toward that end.

Foremost among saints, the Virgin is exalted in the hymns. In the thought of the church the Virgin has held a unique position, unfettered by the restrictions which are common to ordinary mortals. So in the hymns, her virtues admit of no conventional classification. She is the embodiment of an ideal which deepens and broadens in significance as the thoughts of the hymn writers take on the aspects of the age in which they live.

The hymns for the Proper of Saints furnish the complete picture of the ideal Christian warrior, the armies of heaven and the leadership of the angelic hosts. In this connection, the direct influence of the knightly ideal is apparent, supplementing in the thought of contemporary Christianity the ideal of monasticism.

Finally, mention should once more be made of the actual list of virtues and sins which appear to be present to the minds of the hymn writers. The four cardinal virtues appear together. St. Osmund's hymn, *Gaudeamus Messia,* contains the two complete groups of seven sins and seven virtues respectively. Again, the sins which are severely condemned and the virtues which receive the highest praise belong to the standard groups. Avarice is made particularly hateful as well as pride, wrath and envy. Impurity and intemperance are attacked by exalting the ascetic ideal in saintly lives. Incessant activity in the service of God leaves no room for sloth. On the other hand, the principal virtues shine forth in greater clarity than ever, temperance being accounted the most important of the cardinal virtues and faith of the theological virtues, judged by frequency of mention. The great emphasis placed upon faith in all parts of the hymnal has been mentioned elsewhere. This fact supports quite strongly the theory that the Middle Ages were the " ages of faith ", while the absence of any such emphasis upon works will be disappointing to those who hold that faith came into its own with the Reformers of the sixteenth century.

CHAPTER VII

CONCLUSION

ST. AUGUSTINE once defined the hymn as "the praise of God in song."[1]   Rarely has it served this aim alone.   Some additional purpose has moved the author to compose it.   Perhaps, like Ambrose, he has been eager to impress the great doctrines of the church and Christian ideals for daily living. Perhaps, like Fortunatus, he has celebrated the reception of some precious relic.   Perhaps, like Aquinas, he has centered his thought upon a notable feast.   Perhaps like Adam of St. Victor, he has praised God in his saints.   The many and varied aspects of Christian history and experience find place and expression in this literature.   With all ardor and sincerity the author has dwelt upon his immediate theme and purpose, occasionally, it must be admitted, with too little regard for poetic inspiration.   So, in the Middle Ages, the hymns of Latin Christianity made a definite contribution along many lines of thought and, among them, to the teaching of great principles of faith and conduct.

As the various divisions of the liturgical year with its principal feasts pass in review, so the varied aspects of Christian thought and experience find their appropriate places. Throughout the whole, a strong emphasis has been apparent upon ideals of life and conduct, although the emphasis has been uneven, due to the many liturgical phases with which the ethical themes have been interwoven.

[1] *Laus ergo Dei in cantico hymnus dicitur.*   (Commentary on the 148th Psalm, PL, xxxvi, 1948.)

183

A pronounced approval of certain virtues and a corresponding disapproval of certain sins are clearly revealed in medieval hymns. Faith, hope, love, purity, moderation, courage, justice, prudence, humility, and generosity are the great virtues. Pride, impurity, excess, sloth, avarice, wrath, gluttony, and envy are the great sins. These virtues are praised and these sins are scorned, not only as abstract qualities, but in the lives of individuals who embodied them. Persons who have displayed to an unusual degree, one of the chief virtues or the chief sins are held up as types of the specific qualities which distinguish them. Moreover, the emulation of model characters is strongly recommended. Direct teaching by precept or by example is supplemented by the indirect method of attacking a sin by inculcating a love of the opposite virtue. All of the teaching, in so far as it denotes an ethical program, more or less consciously followed, points to the medieval concept of seven principal virtues and seven deadly sins in its larger outlines.

One of the strongest arguments in favor of the theory that such a standard was in the thought of the hymn writers lies in the fact that a very small number of virtues and sins are mentioned apart from those comprised in the lists of seven. When they are found, they are, in almost every case, to be classified in connection with the principal virtues or the deadly sins. Humility, so highly valued, and meekness, a kindred virtue, are the opposites of pride. Generosity is the opposite of avarice. Here the principle of contrast, exhibited likewise in the medieval art which is devoted to the same themes, satisfies the tendency of the mind to seek the opposite idea, and affords a basis for the symbolism of spiritual combat directed against sin. The seven sins and the seven virtues of medieval theology when thus presented, offer a partial satisfaction only, of the desire for contrasts, moderation being opposed to excess and courageous activity to sloth. Consequently, whether humility and generosity are thought of merely as antidotes to pride and avarice, or as weapons to attack them, or as a desirable supplement to contrasts already illustrated in the lists of seven sins and seven virtues, from the point of view of the late Middle Ages it was impossible to dissociate them from the ethical teachings based upon those lists. Other features of the approved life, not definitely included in the list of seven virtues, are found to be parts or aspects of these virtues when they are analyzed.

It is a characteristic feature of ethical and moral teaching in the Middle Ages to provide detailed analyses of good and evil qualities.[1] Several instances of such teaching have been presented in the preceding pages, by way of definition of a specific sin or virtue. So in a number of cases, virtues of the approved life, mentioned in hymns, while not included in the list of seven virtues, are found to be parts or aspects of these virtues when they are analyzed. The wide range of meaning of *temperantia,* for instance, is indicated by Aquinas when he says that this virtue is the curb which should be applied in every case where the passions incite to acts against reason.[2] *Sobrietas* is mentioned by De Burgh and by Angelus de Clavasio as an aspect of *temperantia.*[3] Many other aspects of this virtue are mentioned in various sources but perhaps the most popular form of analyses is that of diagrams of trees of virtues and sins where each of the seven branches has its seven offshoots. Sometimes they were painted on the walls of churches. Often they were drawn in books of devotion. The offshoots of *temperantia* in a diagram from a manuscript psalter of the thirteenth century, are *moralitas, jejunium, sobrietas, contemptus mundi, moder-*

[1] E. L. Cutts, *Parish Priests and Their People,* p. 226.

[2] Aquinas, *Summa,* II, i, 61, 2.

[3] De Burgo, *Pupilla oculi,* p. clxiiii; De Clavasio, *Summa angelica* (Venice, 1486).

atio, benignitas and *tolerantia.*[1]　Here, fasting and the life of poverty should be pointed out as phases of *temperantia.* Patience appears in the same " tree " as an offshoot of hope.　Mercy is an aspect of love just as Aquinas declared it to be when he classified the seven works of mercy, in both their corporal and spiritual forms, under the third of the theological virtues.[2]　Thus the tendency to over-elaboration, so characteristic of medieval analyses of sins and virtues, serves to broaden the meaning of each quality and at the same time, to enable the teacher to gather together a variety of ideas into one general system.　It is conceivable that a modern reader of the hymns might be quite unaware of associations of ideas which to a medieval worshipper were perfectly obvious.　Approaching the literature from a medieval viewpoint, the student is justified in accounting for the mention of some virtue or sin not named in the lists, on the basis of the standards of seven sins and seven virtues as popularly understood in the past.　Moreover, like all rigid systems, the scheme of seven would necessarily require supplement at times to meet the complexities of human experience.　It is quite unnecessary, however, to strain this point, for even if the analyses are ignored entirely, the total number of instances where related virtues are mentioned, excepting humility and generosity, is so infrequent as to be negligible.

Reference has been made in the preceding pages to the relative value attached to certain virtues or sins as revealed by the number of times they appear, irrespective of connotation.　Incidentally, the numerical count of citations related to ethical matters is surprisingly large when one considers the scope and variety of subjects included within the hymn col-

[1] *Vide* Cutts, *op. cit.*, pp. 229, 230.

[2] Aquinas, *Summa*, II, ii, 32.

lections. From the point of view of the actual number of illustrations, faith and love are found to be the most prized of the theological virtues and moderation and courage, of the cardinal virtues. There are fewer references to hope, prudence and justice. The most hated sin is impurity. Pride, wrath and sloth follow closely, and are about evenly stressed. Envy stands next while avarice and gluttony complete the list with the fewest citations. The uneven distribution observable in the case of the sins is corrected by the method of teaching through opposites, by which device avarice and gluttony assume an importance which the numerical count fails to indicate. The total number of references to virtues is much greater than the number of references to sins. In other words the teaching tends to be positive rather than negative. This is true, specifically as well as generally. There are, for instance, a very large number of references to fasting as compared with gluttony. The argument from frequency or infrequency of mention must be employed with caution. It is helpful but not conclusive. The setting of the hymn in which the reference occurs must never be overlooked as an indication of the importance of a particular virtue or sin. This principle of valuation has been followed throughout this study. Hope, justice and prudence, which lag behind faith, love, moderation and courage, in frequency of citation, appear in connotations which greatly enhance their intrinsic value as individual or social ideals. Again, the problem of estimating the extent to which certain virtues are prized or certain sins detested, is much complicated by the poetic medium. A greater insight into the spirit and canons of poetry, especially poetry which possesses a strong emotional character, is a qualification much to be desired by one who would evaluate the moral and ethical standards of Latin hymnology. Looking at the whole problem of the relative importance of specific sins and virtues in the larger perspective which is opened up by the connotation of the hymns, their distribution seems to be maintained in a fairly even proportion.

In reviewing the contributions made to ideals of conduct by hymns occurring in various parts of the liturgy, it should be remembered that groups of hymns which have been discussed separately are found side by side in actual usage. The hymns for the Proper of the Season, the Common of Saints and the Proper of Saints are interwoven, as the services, week by week, are drawn from these three sections of the liturgy. Consequently, the teachings which have been traced, section by section, are presented in practice in a larger unity. With this caution in mind, they may now be summarized in the order which has been followed above. The Proper of the Season includes hymns for the Canonical Hours which place special emphasis upon the virtues of self-control, courage, faith, hope and love, and upon the sins of impurity, sloth, pride and strife; for Advent, exalting humility, faith and hope but condemning wrath and envy, particularly in the person of Herod; for Lent, teaching asceticism with the virtues of purity and abstinence, particularly in food and drink, and the hatred of pride and excess. In the hymns for Lent, the allegorical struggle between good and evil is suggested. Continuing the Proper of the Season, hymns for Easter praise justice, humility and the life of poverty, and condemn pride and avarice, particularly in the person of Judas; hymns for Pentecost exalt love and the seven gifts from which the seven virtues spring; hymns for Trinity and the concluding festivals of the year reveal the importance of faith, hope and love. At Easter and Corpus Christi the theme of spiritual combat appears. The hymns for the Proper of the Season considered as one group reveal the importance attached to the same sins and virtues which belong to the lists of sins and virtues current during the period prior to 1100, in which period, with a very few exceptions, they were written.

The hymns for the Common of Saints are supplementary to those just mentioned, in that they belong to the same period of composition and reflect the same opinion upon the ideal life. The objective ideal is exalted in these hymns, in the persons of the apostles, martyrs, confessors and virgins, the imitation of whom is enjoined. The saints appear as leaders in the spiritual struggle against sin, a theme already treated in a general way. The four cardinal virtues are exalted in these hymns. De Burgh's association of justice with the apostles, courage with the martyrs, prudence with the confessors, and temperance with the virgins, may be fanciful, but the fact remains that the early heroes and heroines of Christian history displayed preeminently the old pagan virtues re-interpreted by those who venerated them.

The hymns for the Proper of Saints present in general the well-rounded treatment of the various themes so far incomplete in other sections of the liturgy. The objective ideal attains its full proportions in the praise of saintly figures who are types of a specific virtue or attitude. St. Stephen is the type of love, St. Peter of faith, St. John the Evangelist of purity, St. John the Baptist of asceticism, St. Andrew of meekness, St. Nicholas of generosity and St. Katherine of the virgin life. Over against these stand the types of sinners, chiefly the persecutors, who are the incarnation of avarice, envy and wrath. Herod had been the first persecutor. He is now followed by Nero, Domitian, Aegeas, Decius and others who are guilty of the same sins. The imitation of the saintly example, as an element in ethical teaching, hitherto commended in a general way, is made specific in this group of hymns and thus intensified in its application. Spiritual conflict is presented on a larger scale with the full participation of the heavenly hosts. St. Michael

the Archangel is discovered as the commander-in-chief of
the celestial ranks with lesser saints in subordinate leadership under whom men may fight with assurance of victory
over sin.   The teaching as to seven sins and seven virtues
is also presented in a complete form.   The theological virtues
grouped together, have not been unusual in the hymns so far
reviewed but the four cardinal virtues are mentioned together for the first time in this division of the liturgy.   All
seven virtues ornament the character of St. Osmund, as the
sequence in his honor makes clear.   The seven sins are defined in a hymn for St. Mary Magdalene, while they are
named in the sequence for St. Osmund just cited.   It is
evident that the hymns for the Proper of Saints are in complete harmony with the ethical opinions found in other forms
of religious literature, and with the teachings conveyed in
secular literature, in drama and in art.   In this respect the
hymns found in the third and final section of the liturgy reveal the fully matured system of seven principal virtues and
seven deadly sins.

So far the hymns of the liturgy have been thought of as
containing the pattern of the ideal life, fitted together bit
by bit, in the order in which the various hymns of the year
make their distinctive contributions.   It is possible to view
the hymns from another angle, as reflecting, not the completed pattern of the ideal life, but the evolution of that ideal.
The pagan virtues, transmitted to Christian thought by men
like Ambrose, characterize the earliest hymns.   They are
simple in expression, direct and objective in the manner of
the Roman mind which interpreted them.   The ideal is
clearly presented in the first morning and evening hymns and
in the hymns praising the early martyrs.   Gradually the
monastic ideal, pervading the whole church, makes its impress upon hymnology.   The spirit and aims of Gregory the
Great illustrate the kind of influence which becomes apparent

at this stage. It has two aspects, that which praises abstinence and renunciation, and that which is felt in the contemplative and subjective side of Christian experience. The old cardinal virtues are the mark of the former, especially in their negative aspects, and the theological virtues the mark of the latter, since faith hope and love are thought of as the conditions of spiritual vision. The monastic ideal becomes valid for clergy and laity alike.

The idea of spiritual warfare was always a feature of Christian teaching from the beginning. To the evolution of the concept of the Christian warrior is due the influence, which to a certain extent, modifies the monastic ideal in hymns. The epic poems of Prudentius first described spiritual warfare as a strife between virtues and vices. The epic type of presentation is not, however, adapted to lyric poetry, and the hymn writers seem to have preferred the symbolism of the Christian warrior contending with sin, as Galahad fought single-handed with the Seven Deadly Sins. Osmund is the counterpart in hymns, of Galahad in the legend, a stainless knight. In some such way may be described the influence of the knightly ideal of contemporaneous society, appearing in hymns with the monastic ideal, not so much its rival as its complement. The saints are now knightly champions. To select a typical historical personage who embodied such a combination of qualities, perhaps Louis IX of France will serve to illustrate the medieval Christian who endeavored to cultivate both aspects of the ideal life as hymns reveal it. The ideal of conduct in its complete evolution is expressed in terms of the society which approved it and in the figure of the knight-monk.

The hymns of Latin Christianity bear a direct relation to medieval opinion upon the subject of ethical ideals, especially as expressed in the system of seven principal virtues and seven deadly sins. The attitude which they display toward each of the hated or approved qualities is unequivocal. An infinite variety of resource is employed to convey their meaning. All the possibilities of liturgical emphasis are brought to bear upon the problem, yet with a surprising freedom from stereotyped phrasing or conventional forms, the cumulative effect of which is the presentation of the medieval conception of the ideal life with remarkable fidelity and forcefulness. It must be admitted, of course, that medieval Christianity received its ideals as a heritage from the past, that these ideals were re-interpreted by medieval philosophers, and perpetuated through all the period by superimposed authority. The hymn was only one medium by which such teachings were spread to the laity.

At the same time it would be false to assume that the ideas of individuals had no share in the process of re-interpretation or that fresh inspiration played no part in their expression. The hymns bear living witness to the actual vitality and growth of certain ideals, exhibited in at least one agency for their diffusion. Hymnology reflects both the inheritance and its accretions because it is a form of social expression. A hymn is essentially communal. It cannot but display the approved ideals of the society which uses it, in a form which manifests the characteristic attitude of that society toward the inheritance which is tacitly accepted. By its very nature the hymn is adapted to show forth the aspirations not only of individuals momentarily united but the deeper forces of thought and emotion which are shared reciprocally. " The lyric of the hymns exalts the common emotions of common observance. It is the poetry of aspirations shared not only with all Christians everywhere, but with immediate companions turning work into worship. It expresses the visions of a fellowship." [1]   Herein lies one explanation of the

[1] C. S. Baldwin, *Medieval Rhetoric and Poetic* (N. Y.: Macmillan Co., 1928), p. 123.

statement which Father Blume has made in the lines with which this essay opens. The culture and spiritual life of the Middle Ages are reflected in its religious lyric poetry. If it did not reflect that standard of ethics which commended itself to medieval thought, it would deny the forces of social psychology which produced it, for a long process of development lies behind the various manifestations of the ideal which the hymns set forth. An objective description of these manifestations is only one way of accounting for the existence of the ideal in perfected form. There still remains the subjective point of view, the inner evolution of feeling, of appreciation, of emotion which has contributed to its full maturity. True, the subjective aspect may vary and does vary, in the men who value the ideal and in the successive periods in which it finds expression. Still the contributions of each personality and of each age are combined into a whole which possesses a constant quality and an appeal which continues to be irresistible from first to last. Here the boundary line is crossed between the individual and the social, as the common life of men together not only reinforces and augments, but itself may create the ideal life of the group.[1]

The religious life of the Middle Ages, better perhaps than any other aspect of the period, illustrates the weight of the social factor and the unconscious process by which ethical and moral ideals were shaped and influenced. As an American sociologist has expressed it, " If certain ways of feeling become traditional and are fostered by customs, symbols, and the cult of examples, they may rise to a high level in many individuals. In this way sentiment, even passion, may have

---

[1] "La société est essentiellement créatrice d'idéal. Par ses propriétés, par les forces propres qui se dégagent de la réunion des hommes, s'expliquent les caractères de ces grands aiments qu'on appelle les valeurs." C. Bouglé, *Leçons de Sociologie sur l'Évolution des Valeurs* (Paris: Colin, 1922), p. 15.

an institutional character.   Of this too the various phases
of medieval Christianity afford examples." [1]   So the ideals
which were evolved from the concept of deadly sins and principal virtues functioned as actual forces in medieval society,
at once the creation of that society which cherished them and
a guide to its further moral progress.

When Christianity came to the parting of the ways in the
sixteenth century, the scheme of seven sins and seven virtues
was abandoned by the reformed churches.   But the medieval
tradition based on scholastic teachings lived on in the Roman
church and to this day, in addition to the decalogue, is valid for
Catholicism everywhere.   For Protestantism the decalogue
became the basis of ethical teachings. [2]   If further evidence
were needed to support the view that hymnology follows the
ideas of the age, it could be found in the fact that the Catholic
church retained its traditional hymnology, excepting the
sequence, [3] while in the Protestant churches a multitude of
new hymns sprang up which were the appropriate expression
of their purposes and ideals.

[1] C. H. Cooley, *Social Process* (N. Y.: Scribners, 1920), p. 25.

[2] O. Zöckler, *Tugendlehre*, p. 304; *Lehrstück von den sieben Hauptsünden*, p. 98.

[3] Four sequences only were retained in the revised Roman missal of
1570, namely, *Victimae paschali, Veni sancte spiritus, Lauda Sion salvatorem* and *Dies irae dies illa.   Stabat mater dolorosa* was added about
1727.   *Vide* Julian, p. 1042.

BIBLIOGRAPHY

I. Bibliographies

Leclercq, L., Article "Hymnes", *Dictionnaire d'archéologie chrétienne et de liturgie.* Contains extensive bibliography upon the subject of medieval hymnology.

Raby, F. J. E., *History of Christian-Latin poetry from the beginning to the close of the Middle Ages.* Oxford, 1927. Contains extensive bibliography classified by authors and periods.

II. Collections and Indices

Analecta hymnica medii aevi, edited by C. Blume and G. M. Dreves, 55 vols. Leipzig, 1886-1922.

Analecta liturgica, part 2, vols. I, *Thesaurus hymnologicus*; II, *Prosae*, edited by E. Misset and W. H. J. Weale. Insulis et Brugis, 1888-1902.

Blume, C. and Dreves, G. M., *Hymnologische Beiträge* (Quellen und Forschungen zur Geschichte der lateinischen Hymnendichtungen, 2 vols.). Leipzig, 1897-1901.

Chevalier, C. U. J., *Repertorium hymnologicum*, catalogue des chants, hymnes, proses, sequences, tropes, 6 vols. Louvain, Bruxelles, 1892-1920. Published as supplements to the *Analecta Bollandiana.*

Daniel, H. A., *Thesaurus hymnologicus*, 5 vols. Lipsiae, 1855-1856. 2nd edition.

Kehrein, J., *Lateinische Sequenzen des Mittelalters*. Mainz, 1873. The most extensive collection of sequences made up to that date.

Mearns, J., *Early Latin hymnaries*, an index of hymns in hymnaries before 1100, with an appendix from later sources. Cambridge, 1913.

Mone, F. J., *Lateinische Hymnen des Mittelalters*, 3 vols. Freiburg im Breisgau, 1853-1855.

Morel, G., *Lateinische Hymnen des Mittelalters*, grösstentheils aus Handschriften schweizerischen Klöster, als Nachtrag zu den Hymnensammlungen von Mone, Daniel and Andern. Einsiedeln, 1866.

Neale, J. M., *Sequentiae ex missalibus Germanicis, Anglicis, Gallicis, aliisque medii aevi, collectae.* London, 1852.

Roth, F. W. E., *Lateinische Hymnen des Mittelalters*. Augsburg, 1887. Intended as a supplement to larger collections.

Wackernagel, K. E., *Das deutschen Kirchenlied*, 5 vols. Leipzig, 1864-1877. Vol. I contains Latin hymns.

Walpole, A. S., *Early Latin hymns*. Cambridge, 1922.

III. History of Latin Hymns

Baldwin, C. S., *Medieval rhetoric and poetic.* New York, 1928.

Dreves, G. M., *Ein Jahrtausend lateinischer Hymnendichtung,* Eine
Blütenlese aus den Anal. hymn. mit literarhistorischen Erläuterungen,
2 vols. Leipzig, 1909.

Duffield, S. W., *The Latin hymn-writers and their hymns.* New York,
1889.

Ebert, Ad., *Allgemeine Geschichte der Literatur des Mittelalters im
Abendlande,* 3 vols. Leipzig, 1880-1889. 2nd edition of vol. I.

Gautier, L., *Oeuvres poétiques d'Adam de Saint-Victor.* Paris, 1881.

Julian, J., *Dictionary of Hymnology.* London, 1925.

Kayser, J., *Beiträge zur Geschichte und Erklärung der ältesten Kirchen-
hymnen,* 2 vols. Paderborn, 1881, 1886.

Labriolle, P. de, *Histoire de la littérature latine chrétienne.* Paris 1924.
2nd edition. The period up to 600 A. D. is covered.

Mac Gilton, A. K., *Study of Latin hymns.* Boston, 1918. Brief popular
study with index showing where many hymns may be found in the
great collections.

Manitius, M., *Geschichte der lateinischen Literatur des Mittelalters,* Parts
I, II. München, 1911-1923.

Manitius, M., *Geschichte der christlich-lateinischen Poesie bis zur Mitte
des 8. Jahrhunderts.* Stuttgart, 1891.

Misset, E., et Aubry, P., *Les Proses d'Adam de Saint-Victor,* texte et
musique. Paris, 1900. This is a beautifully arranged critical edition.

Rand, E. K., *Founders of the Middle Ages.* Cambridge, 1928.

Trench, R. C., *Sacred Latin Poetry.* London, 1874.

IV. Liturgical Hymns and Medieval Liturgies in England

Blume, C., *Hymnologische Beiträge* (Der Cursus S. Benedicti Nursini
und die liturgischen Hymnen des 6.-9. Jahrhunderts), 3. Band.
Leipzig, 1908.

Britt, M., *Hymns of the breviary and missal.* New York, 1922. Modern
use.

Dowden, J., *Church year and kalendar.* Cambridge, 1910.

Fisher, A. H., *Cathedral church of Hereford.* London, 1898.

Frere, W. H., "Introduction" in *Hymns, ancient and modern.* London,
1909. The history of Latin hymns is treated from the liturgical
point of view.

——, *Winchester troper.* London, 1894. (Henry Bradshaw Society
Pub., vol. VIII).

Gautier, L., *Histoire de la poésie liturgique au moyen âge. Les tropes.*
Paris, 1886.

Hoskins, E., *Horae beatae Mariae virginis or Sarum and York Primers.*
London, 1901.

Hymnale secundum usum insignis ac praeclarae ecclesiae Sarisburiensis, edited by Wilson and Stubbs. Littlemore, 1850.

Hymnarium Sarisburiense. London, 1851. Incomplete.

Hymner, Translations of the hymns from the Sarum breviary together with sundry sequences and processions. London, 1905.

Jones, W. H., *Salisbury.* London, 1880. (Diocesan histories.)

Maskell, W., *Ancient liturgy of the church of England.* Oxford, 1882. 3rd edition.

Maskell, W., *Monumenta ritualia ecclesiae Anglicanae,* 3 vols. Oxford, 1882. 2nd edition.

Newman, J. H., *Hymni ecclesiae.* London, 1865. These hymns are chosen chiefly from the Paris, Roman, Salisbury and York breviaries.

Ornsby, G., *York.* London, no date. (Diocesan histories.)

Phillott, H. W., *Hereford.* London, no date. (Diocesan histories.)

Raine, J., *York.* London, 1893.

Rock, D., *Church of our fathers as seen in St. Osmund's rite for the cathedral of Salisbury,* 4 vols. Edited by G. W. Hart and W. H. Frere. London, 1903-1904.

Sarum missal, edited by J. W. Legg. Oxford, 1916.

Sarum missal, done into English by A. H. Pearson. London, 1884. 2nd edition.

Sarum missal, translated by F. E. Warren. London, 1911. (Library of liturgiology and ecclesiology for English readers, vols. 8 and 9.)

Swete, H. B., *Church services and service books before the Reformation.* London, 1896.

Thalhofer, V. and Eisenhofer, L., *Handbuch der katholischen Liturgik,* 2 vols. Freiburg im Breisgau, 1912. 2nd edition.

Wordsworth, C., *Notes on mediaeval services in England.* London, 1898.

Wordsworth, C. and Littlehales, H., *The old service books of the English church.* London, 1904.

Note: Names of books given with the table of abbreviations are not repeated above.

V. General Works Useful in Studying the Connection Between Art, Drama, Culture and Hymns in the Middle Ages

Back, F., *Mittelrheinische Kunst; Beiträge zur Geschichte der Malerei und Plastik in 14.-15. Jahrhundert.* Frankfurt, 1910.

Blume, C., "Hymnologie und Kulturgeschichte des Mittelalters," in *Festschrift f. Georg von Hertling.* Kempten, 1913. Pp. 117-130.

Bremond, H., *Sainte Catherine d'Alexandrie.* Paris, no date. L'Art et les saints.

Chambers, E. K., *Mediaeval stage,* 2 vols. Oxford, 1903.

Clement, C. E., *Handbook of legendary and mythological art*. Boston, 1881.

Coffman, G. R., "A new approach to mediaeval Latin drama", *Modern Philology*, XXII (1925), pp. 239-271.

Cohen, G., *Histoire de la mise en scene dans le theatre religieux français du moyen âge*. Paris, 1926. Contains a remarkably fine bibliography.

Creizenach, W., *Geschichte des neueren Dramas*. Halle, 1911. Vol. I.

Ditchfield, P. H., *Cathedrals of Gt. Britain*. London, 1916.

Drake, M. & W., *Saints and their emblems*. London, 1916.

Duchartre, P. L., *Mittelalterliche Plastik in Frankreich*. München, 1925.

Gautier, L., *La poésie religieuse dans les cloîtres des IXe-XIe siècles*. Paris, 1887.

Jameson, A. M., *Sacred and legendary art*. London, 1866. 5th edition.

Kretzmann, P. E., *The liturgical element in the earliest forms of the medieval drama*. (Univ. of Minn. studies in language and literature, no. 4, 1916). Special reference is made to the plays of England and Germany.

Künstle, K., *Ikonographie der Heiligen*. Freiburg im Breisgau, 1926.

Mâle, E., *L'art religieux du XIIe siècle en France*. Paris, 1922.

——, *L'art religieux du XIIIe siècle en France*. Paris, 1923. 5th edition.

——, *L'art religieux de la fin du moyen âge en France*. Paris, 1922. 2nd edition.

——, *L'art allemand et l'art français du moyen âge*. Paris, 1923. 4th edition.

Marguillier, A., *Saint Nicolas*. Paris, no date. L'art et les saints.

Muller, H. F., "Pre-history of the mediaeval drama", *Zeitschrift für romanische Philologie*, Bd. 44 (1924), pp. 544-575. The antecedents of the tropes and the conditions of their appearance.

Nelson, P., *Ancient stained glass in England*. London, 1913.

Prior, E. A. and Gardner, A., *An account of medieval figure-sculpture in England*. Cambridge, 1912.

Stroppel, R., *Liturgie und geistliche Dichtung zwischen 1050-1300*. Frankfurt am Main, 1927. German vernacular poetry.

Vitry, P., et Brière, G., *Documents de sculpture française du moyen âge*. Paris, no date.

VI. General Works Useful in Studying the Connection Between Cults of Saints and Hymns

Acta sanctorum quotquot orbe coluntur . . . collegit Joannes Bollandus etc., 1643 *et seq.*

Ante-Nicene Fathers, vol. VII, American reprint. Buffalo, 1886. This volume contains the apocryphal books of the New Testament.

Arnold-Forster, F., *Studies in church dedications*, 3 vols. London, 1879.

Beissel, S., *Geschichte der Verehrung Marias in Deutschland während des Mittelalters* (*Stimmen aus Maria-Laach*, vol. 66). Freiburg im Breisgau, 1896.

——, *Verehrung der Heiligen und ihrer Reliquien in Deutschland bis zum Beginne des 13. Jahrhundert* (*Stimmen aus Maria-Laach*, vol. 47). Freiburg im Breisgau, 1890.

——, *Verehrung der Heiligen und ihrer Reliquien in Deutschland während der zweiten Hälfte des Mittelalters* (*Stimmen aus Maria-Laach*, vol. 54). Freiburg im Breisgau, 1892.

Bridgett, J. E., *Our Lady's Dowry.* London, no date.

Delehaye, H., *Les légendes hagiographiques.* Bruxelles, 1905.

Gerould, G. H., *Saints' legends.* Boston, 1916. A history of saints' lives as they have appeared in English literature.

Jacopo de Voragine, *Golden legend.* Lives of the saints as Englished by William Caxton, 7 vols. *Temple classics*, edited by F. S. Ellis. London, 1900.

Kirsch, J. P., *Doctrine of the communion of saints in the ancient church*, translated by J. R. M'Kee. Edinburgh, c. 1910. For early aspects of the Virgin cult.

Lucius, E., *Die Anfänge des Heiligen-kults in der christlichen Kirche.* Tübingen, 1904.

Stanton, R., *Menology of England and Wales.* London, 1892.

VII. MEDIEVAL BOOKS OF POPULAR DEVOTION AND RELIGIOUS INSTRUCTION. THE SEVEN SINS AND THE SEVEN VIRTUES

Berthold of Regensburg, *Predigten*, 2 vols. Edited by F. Pfeiffer & Strobl. Wien, 1862-1880.

Bohatta, H., *Bibliographie der livres d'heures* (*horae B. M. V.*), *officia, hortuli animae, coronae B. M. V., ... des XV. & XVI. Jahrhunderts.* Wien, 1924. 2nd edition.

Brown, C., *English religious lyrics of the 14th century.* Oxford, 1924.

——, *Register of middle English religious and didactic verse.* Oxford, 1920. Pt. II.

Cutts, E. L., *Parish priests and their people in the Middle Ages.* London, 1918. 2nd edition.

Dittrich, O., *Geschichte der Ethik*, 3 vols. Leipzig, 1926.

Étienne de Bourbon, *Anecdotes historiques*, edited by A. Lecoy de la Marche. Paris, 1877. (Publications de la société de l'histoire de France.)

Gasquet, F. A., *Parish life in mediaeval England.* London, 1907.

Gesta Romanorum, edited by H. Oesterley. Berlin, 1872. English translation by Swan & Hooper. London, 1904. (Bohn's antiquarian library.)

Hall, T. C., *History of ethics within organized Christianity*. New York, 1910.

Jacques de Vitry, *Exempla*, edited by T. F. Crane. London, 1890. (Folk-lore society publications, vol. 26.)

Joannes de Burgo, *Pupilla oculi*. Strassburg, 1517.

Lay folks' catechism, edited by Simmons and Nolloth. (Early English text society, old series, vol. 118.)

Michael, E., *Geschichte des deutschen Volkes seitdem 13. Jahr. bis zum Ausgang des Mittelalters*, 6 vols. Freiburg, 1897-1915.

Mosher, J. A., *The Exemplum in the early religious and didactic literature of England*. New York, 1911.

Myrc, J., *Festiall*. (Early English text society, ext. series, vol. 96.)

——, *Instructions for parish priests*. (Early English text society, old series, vol. 31.)

Owst, G. R., *Preaching in medieval England*. Cambridge, 1926. Covers the period between 1350-1450.

Robert Manning of Brunne, *Handlyng synne*. (Early English text society, old series, vols. 119, 123.)

Smith, H. P., *Essays in Biblical interpretation*. Boston, 1921.

Strong, T. B., *Christian ethics*. London, 1896.

Villien, A., *Histoire des commandements de l'église*. Paris, 1909.

Wells, J. E., *Manual of the writings in middle English,* 1050-1400. New Haven, 1916.

Zöckler, O., *Das Lehrstück v. d. 7 Hauptsünden*. München, 1893.

——, *Die Tugendlehre des Christentums*. Gütersloh, 1904.

INDEX OF FIRST LINES OF HYMNS

GENERAL INDEX

Abstinence, 65, 88, 89, 93, 112, 124, 154, 188, 191

Activity, 63, 74, 88, 112, 184

Adam of St. Victor, 43, 109, 148, 183

Advent, 82, 88, 101; ideals in hymns of, 112; 188

Aegeas, 131, 189

Agatha, St., 123, 157, 158, 161

Agnes, St., 123, 157, 164

Alan of Lille, 36, 176

Albertus Magnus, 149

Alcuin, 51, 94

Aldhelm, 175

Alexander of Hales, 168

All Saints, 129, 165; ideals in hymns for, 166, 167

Allegory, 15; poems of Prudentius, 73; *vide* spiritual warfare

Ambrose, St., 39; concerning hour services, 61; as a hymn writer, 63, 69, 72, 73; cardinal virtues, 77; *De officiis,* 77; *De Paradiso,* 77; 83, 114; *De virginibus,* 125, 148; 134, 183, 190

Andrew, St., 23, 117; type of meekness, 130, 131, 133, 181, 189

Anne, St., 136

Annunciation, 146

Anselm of Canterbury, 149

Anthony the Hermit, St., 152, 154

Anticlaudianus, 176

Apocryphal Gospels, 144

Apostles, 115, 127, 130, 140, 166, 189; as judges, 117-118; as leaders in spiritual warfare, 116; as types of justice, 125, 126

Aquinas, Thomas, defines justification, 100; hymns of, 109; on the sins, 168; on the virtues, 174; 183, 185, 186

Archangels, as leaders in spiritual warfare, 139, 140, 141

Aristotle, 76, 100

Armagillus, St., 158

Art, 17, 190; St. Michael in, 140;

saints as knights in, 141; St. Katherine in, 156; St. Nicholas in, 160; sins and virtues in, 178-180

Ascension, 96, 102, 165

Assumption of the Blessed Virgin, 147

Augustine, St., on hymns of Ambrose, 72; on the virtues, 77; on the sins, 80, 93; on St. Paul, 117; defines *hymn,* 182

Augustine of Canterbury, St., 41, 50, 153

Avarice, 14, 74; in early lists of sins, 78, 79, 80, 93, 95; the sin of Judas, 99; 158, 159, 163; in later lists of sins, 168; 181, 182, 184, 185, 187, 188

Ayenbite of Inwyt, 30, 171, 178

Barbara, St., 123, 156

Bede, 74, 76, 94, 146

Benedict, St., 41, 152, 157, 158, 163

Benedictine Rule, 41

Bernard of Clairvaux, St., 35, 149, 162

Berthold of Regensburg, 173, 174, 175

Boasting, 69, 95, 112

Bonaventura, 105, 168

Book of Hours, vide Prymer

Bosworth Psalter, 42

Bravery; *vide* Courage

Buch der Rügen, 36

Caesarius of Heisterbach, 168

Canonical hours, origin of, 59; ideals in hour hymns, 73, 74, 112, 188

Canterbury Tales, 32, 176

Cardinal virtues, in lists of virtues, 76, 77, 81; in hymns for P. of Season, 92, 103, 104, 113; in hymns for C. of Saints, 127; in hymns for P. of Saints, 131, 132, 147, 149; 182, 187, 189, 190, 191

Carmina Burana, 21, 99
Cassian of Marseilles, 80, 90; his list of sins, 80, 93, 94
Caswall, Edward, 18, 46
Cecilia, St., 123
Chansons de Geste, 102
Chastity, 89, 91, 109, 122, 126, 135, 142, 148
Church attendance, 31, 32, 34, 36; obligation to attend Mass, 32, 33; canonical hours attended by laymen, 60
Cicero, 78
Clement of Alexandria, 77
Collationes of Cassian, 80
Compline, 59; hymns for, 68
Confessors, 115, 116; virtues of, 121, 122, 125; types of prudence, 126; 127, 128, 166, 189
Corpus Christi, 108, 110, 113, 188
Courage (or bravery), 16; in Hour hymns, 63, 74; a cardinal virtue, 76, 78; in hymns for P. of Season, 97, 109, 113; in hymns for C. of Saints, 116, 118, 120, 123, 125, 128; in hymns for P. of Saints, 132, 149, 166; 184, 187, 188; *vide* also Fortitude.
Covetousness, 30, 79
Cruelty, 85, 88, 112, 113, 127
Cuthbert, St., 51, 154, 157

Dan Michel of Northgate, 171
Dante, 161, 177
De ecclesiasticis disciplinis, 94
De institutis coenobiorum, 80
De laudibus Mariae Virginis, 149
De octo vitiis principalibus, 175
Decalogue, 79, 94, 194
Deceit, 64, 85, 95, 113
Decius, 159, 161, 189
Dedication of a Church, 108, 113
Denis, St., 157
Desert of Religion, 178
Domitian, 136, 189
Drama, 17, 20, 24, 190; liturgical, 84, 87, 97; secular, 177; moralities, 177; Corpus Christi cycles, 177; Pater Noster Plays, 177; St. Katherine in, 156; as an aid to religious education, 177, 178
Durandus, Guilelmus, 61
Durham Hymnarium, 47

Easter, 97, 99, 108; ideals in hymns for, 113; 165, 188

Edmund, St., 157
Egbert, archbishop of York, 51, 94
Envy, 16, 30; in Hour hymns, 74, 75; in early lists of sins, 78, 79, 93, 95; in hymns for P. of Season, 85, 88, 112, 113; in hymns for P. of Saints, 161, 162; 163; in later lists of sins, 167; 182, 184, 187, 188
Epiphany, 87, 88
Ethelbert, St., 53, 154
Ethelwold, St., 126, 154, 157, 158, 163
Étienne de Bourbon, 34, 172
Eugenius of Toledo, 74, 76
Evagrius Ponticus, 79, 80
Evensong, *vide* Vespers
Exempla, 171, 172
Expositio hymnorum et sequentiarum, 46

Faith, 16; in Hour hymns, 65, 66, 69, 74; a theological virtue, 77, 78, 81; in hymns for P. of Season, 88, 99, 108, 109, 112, 113, 114; in hymns for C. of Saints, 118, 119, 121, 122, 124, 128; in hymns for P. of Saints, 131, 132, 134, 142, 146, 147, 149, 157, 163, 164, 166, 182, 184, 187, 188
Fasting, 36, 88, 90, 122, 124, 154, 186, 187
Fortitude, 61; in hymns for P. of Season, 103, 113; in hymns for C. of Saints, 119, 120, 121, 122, 123, 124, 126; in hymns for P. of Saints, 136, 153, 156
Fortunatus, 83, 97, 183
François Villon, 35
Fulbert of Chartres, 97

Gabriel, St., 139, 140, 146
Galahad, 142, 191
Generosity, 158, 159, 160, 161, 180, 181, 184, 185
Geneviève, St., 154
Gesta Romanorum, 176
Gluttony, 16, 30; in Hour hymns, 74, 75; in early lists of sins, 79, 80, 93, 95; in hymns for P. of Season, 89, 90, 113; in hymns for P. of Saints, 163; in later lists of sins, 168; 184, 187
Golden Legend, 23, 144, 155, 159
Goliardic poetry, 20, 21

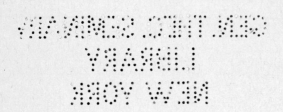